CUTE & CUDDLY
CROSS STITCH

Cute & Cuddly

CROSS STITCH

JANE ALFORD • GAIL BUSSI • DOROTHEA HALL
JULIE HASLER • SUSIE JOHNS • CHRISTINA MARSH

MEREHURST

The projects in this book were all stitched with DMC stranded cotton
embroidery threads with the exception of projects on the following
pages, which were stitched with Anchor stranded cotton embroidery threads:
pp 28-31, 34-37 and 106-109.
The keys given with each chart also list combinations for those who wish to use
Anchor or Madeira threads. It should be pointed out that the shades produced by
different companies vary slightly, and it is not always possible to find identical
colours in a different range.

Published in 1995 by Merehurst Limited
Ferry House, 51-57 Lacy Road, Putney, London SW15 1PR
Text and charts on pages 16-17 © copyright Jane Alford,
on pages 12-13, 24-25, 32-33, 40-41, 48-49, 52-53, 64-69, 72-73, 80-81, 84-85,
96-97, 100-101, 104-105, 112-113, 116-117, 124-125, 128-129, 132-133,
136-137, 140-141 © copyright Julie Hasler
© copyright 1995 Merehurst Limited
ISBN 1 853914 89 4

A catalogue record for this book is available from the British Library.

Managing Editor Diana Lodge
Edited by Heather Dewhurst and Diana Lodge
Designed by Maggie Aldred and Sheila Volpe
Photography by Marie Louise Avery (pages 10, 26, 34, 42, 50,
54, 58, 62, 66, 86, 90, 102, 106, 110, 114, 118, 122, 126, 134, and 138),
Di Lewis (page 74) and Debbie Patterson (pages 14, 18, 22, 30, 38, 46, 70, 78, 82, 94, 98 and 130)
Illustrations by John Hutchinson
Typesetting by Dacorum Type & Print, Hemel Hempstead
Colour separation by Fotographics Limited, UK – Hong Kong
Printed in Singapore by Toppan Printing Co.

*Merehurst is the leading publisher of craft books and has an excellent range
of titles to suit all levels. Please send to the address above for our
free catalogue, stating the title of this book.*

CONTENTS

INTRODUCTION

A host of cute and cuddly animals fill the pages of this charming collection of cross stitch designs, intended for young and old alike. For cat lovers, there are beautifully observed portraits of their favourite animal, including a knitting bag with three kittens tangling themselves in a skein of wool and a nightdress case with a picture of a sleeping cat; for those of us who have remained loyal to their teddies, there is a charming assortment of chubby bears decorating a variety of projects, and there are many other adorable animals, making this a group of 'cuddlies' that few will be able to resist.

Each design is featured in a full colour photograph, and accompanied by a chart, together with full instructions for making up the finished article. If you are new to cross stitch you will find that is is one of the most basic and easy-to-master embroidery stitches, and the Basic Skills section covers all the information that you will need, from how to prepare your fabric and stretch it in an embroidery frame to mounting your finished work, ready for display.

As well as many designs that are suitable for beginners, there is also a wide range that will challenge the more experienced cross stitchers.

Whether you are embroidering simply for your own pleasure, or to make lovely gifts for your family and friends, you will find plenty of projects here to excite your interest and provide hours of stitching enjoyment.

BASIC SKILLS

BEFORE YOU BEGIN

PREPARING THE FABRIC
Even with an average amount of handling, many evenweave fabrics tend to fray at the edges, so it is a good idea to overcast the raw edges, using ordinary sewing thread, before you begin.

THE INSTRUCTIONS
Each project begins with a full list of the materials that you will require. All the designs are worked on evenweave fabrics, including Aida, produced by Zweigart. The measurements given for the embroidery fabric include a minimum of 5cm (2in) all around, to allow for stretching it in a frame and preparing the edges to prevent them from fraying.

Colour keys for stranded embroidery cottons – DMC, Anchor or Madeira – are given with each chart. It is assumed that you will need to buy one skein of each colour mentioned in a particular key even though you may use less, but where two or more skeins are needed, this information is included in the main list of requirements.

To work from the charts, particularly those where several symbols are used in close proximity, some readers may find it helpful to have the chart enlarged so that the squares and symbols can be seen more easily. Many photocopying services will do this for a minimum charge.

Before you begin to embroider, always mark the centre of the design with two lines of basting stitches, one vertical and one horizontal, running from edge to edge of the fabric, as indicated by the arrows on the charts.

As you stitch, use the centre lines given on the chart and the basting threads on your fabric as reference points for counting the squares and threads to position your design accurately.

WORKING IN A HOOP
A hoop is the most popular frame for use with small areas of embroidery. It consists of two rings, one fitted inside the other; the outer ring usually has an adjustable screw attachment so that it can be tightened to hold the stretched fabric in place.

Hoops are available in several sizes, ranging from 10cm (4in) in diameter to quilting hoops with a diameter of 38cm (15in). Hoops with table stands or floor stands attached are also available.

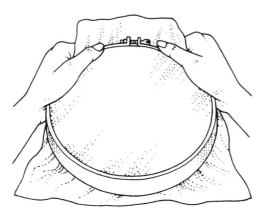

1 To stretch your fabric in a hoop, place the area to be embroidered over the inner ring and press the outer ring over it, with the tension screw released. Tissue paper can be placed between the outer ring and the embroidery, so that the hoop does not mark the fabric. Lay the tissue paper over the fabric when you set it in the hoop, then tear away the central embroidery area.

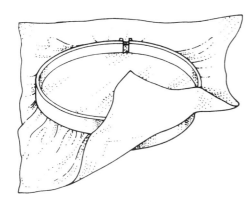

2 Smooth the fabric and, if necessary, straighten the grain before tightening the screw. The fabric should be evenly stretched.

WORKING IN A RECTANGULAR FRAME
Rectangular frames are more suitable for larger pieces of embroidery. They consist of two rollers, with tapes attached, and two flat side pieces, which slot into the rollers and are held in place by pegs or screw attachments. Available in different sizes, either alone or with adjustable table or floor stands, frames are measured by the length of the roller tape,

and range in size from 30cm (12in) to 68cm (27in).

As alternatives to a slate frame, canvas stretchers and the backs of old picture frames can be used. Provided there is sufficient extra fabric around the finished size of the embroidery, the edges can be turned under and simply attached with drawing pins (thumb tacks) or staples.

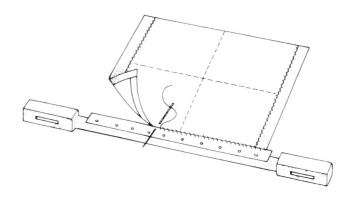

1 To stretch your fabric in a rectangular frame, cut out the fabric, allowing at least an extra 5cm (2in) all around the finished size of the embroidery. Baste a single 12mm (½in) turning on the top and bottom edges and oversew strong tape, 2.5cm (1in) wide, to the other two sides. Mark the centre line both ways with basting stitches. Working from the centre outward and using strong thread, oversew the top and bottom edges to the roller tapes. Fit the side pieces into the slots, and roll any extra fabric on one roller until the fabric is taut.

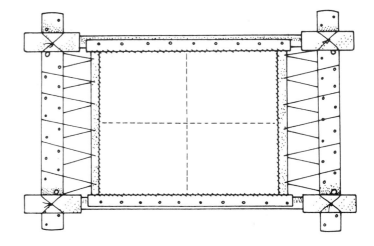

2 Insert the pegs or adjust the screw attachments to secure the frame. Thread a large-eyed needle (chenille needle) with strong thread or fine string and lace both edges, securing the ends around the intersections of the frame. Lace the webbing at 2.5cm (1in) intervals, stretching the fabric evenly.

EXTENDING EMBROIDERY FABRIC

It is easy to extend a piece of embroidery fabric, such as a bookmark, to stretch it in a hoop.

● Fabric oddments of a similar weight can be used. Simply cut four pieces to size (in other words, to the measurement that will fit both the embroidery fabric and your hoop) and baste them to each side of the embroidery fabric before stretching it in the hoop in the usual way.

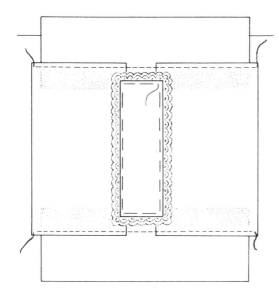

THE STITCHES

CROSS STITCH

For all cross stitch embroidery, the following two methods of working are used. In each case, neat rows of vertical stitches are produced on the back of the fabric.

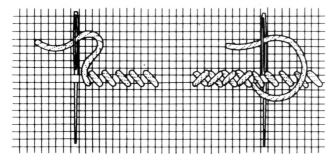

● When stitching large areas, work in horizontal rows. Working from right to left, complete the first row of evenly spaced diagonal stitches over the number of threads specified in the project instructions. Then, working from left to right, repeat the process. Continue in this way, making sure each stitch crosses in the same direction.

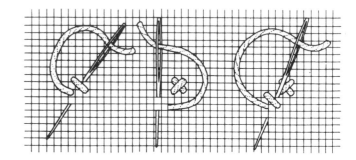

● When stitching diagonal lines, work downwards, completing each stitch before moving to the next.

THREE-QUARTER CROSS STITCHES

Some fractional stitches are used on certain projects in this book; although they strike fear into the hearts of less experienced stitchers they are not difficult to master, and give a more natural line in certain instances. Should you find it difficult to pierce the centre of the Aida block, simply use a sharp needle to make a small hole in the centre first.

To work a three-quarter cross, bring the needle up at point A and down through the centre of the square at B. Later, the diagonal back stitch finishes the stitch. A chart square with two different symbols separated by a diagonal line requires two 'three-quarter' stitches. Backstitch will later finish the square.

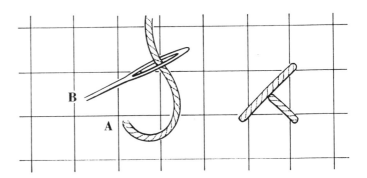

A clear distinction needs to be made between three-quarter stitches and half cross stitches. A three-quarter stitch occupies half of a square diagonally. A half cross stitch is like a normal cross stitch, but only the top stitch is worked, to give a more delicate effect. Stitches worked in this way are indicated quite clearly on the colour keys with their own symbols.

BACKSTITCH

Backstitch is used in the projects to give emphasis to a particular foldline, an outline or a shadow. The stitches are worked over the same number of threads as the cross stitch, forming continuous straight or diagonal lines.

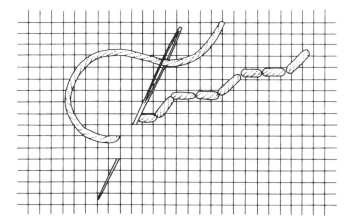

● Make the first stitch from left to right; pass the needle behind the fabric and bring it out one stitch length ahead to the left. Repeat and continue in this way along the line.

FRENCH KNOTS

This stitch is shown on some of the diagrams by a small dot. Where there are several french knots, the dots have been omitted to avoid confusion. Where this occurs you should refer to the instructions of the project and the colour photograph.

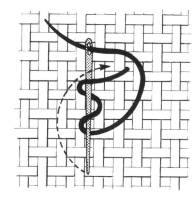

To work a french knot, bring your needle and cotton out slightly to the right of where you want your knot to be. Wind the thread once or twice around the needle, depending on how big you want your knot to be, and insert the needle to the left of the point where you brought it out.

Be careful not to pull too hard or the knot will disappear through the fabric. The instructions state the number of strands of cotton to be used for the french knots.

FINISHING

MOUNTING EMBROIDERY

The cardboard should be cut to the size of the finished embroidery, with an extra 6mm (¼in) added all round to allow for the recess in the frame.

LIGHTWEIGHT FABRICS

1 Place embroidery face down, with the cardboard centred on top, and basting and pencil lines matching. Begin by folding over the fabric at each corner and securing it with masking tape.

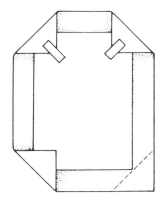 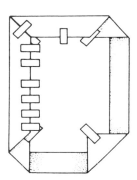

2 Working first on one side and then the other, fold over the fabric on all sides and secure it firmly with pieces of masking tape, placed about 2.5cm (1in) apart. Also neaten the mitred corners with masking tape, pulling the fabric tightly to give a firm, smooth finish.

HEAVIER FABRICS

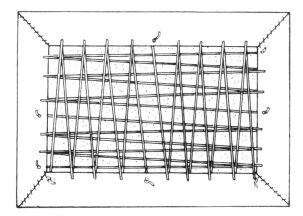

● Lay the embroidery face down, with the cardboard centred on top; fold over the edges of the fabric on opposite sides, making mitred folds at the corners, and lace across, using strong thread. Repeat on the other two sides. Finally, pull up the fabric firmly over the cardboard. Overstitch the mitred corners.

9

PICTURES AND SAMPLERS

One of the delights of cross stitch, as embroiderers discovered many centuries ago, is that it can be used to create pictures which may be complex, like the portrait of three kittens featured here, or bold and simple, like the children's samplers that follow. The teddy pictures would delight any small child, while the country mice could creep into almost any room in your home.

THREE IN A ROW

YOU WILL NEED

For the picture, measuring 42cm × 37cm
(16½in × 14½in) unframed:

*50cm × 45cm (20in × 18in) of cream, 28-count
Quaker cloth
Stranded embroidery cotton in the colours given in
the panel
No26 tapestry needle
42cm × 37cm (16½in × 14½in) of mounting
board
Picture frame of your choice*

•

THE EMBROIDERY

Prepare the fabric and stretch it in a frame (see page 7). Following the chart, start the embroidery at the centre of the design, using two strands of thread in the needle and making each cross stitch over two fabric threads. Finish by backstitching around the eyes, using one strand of thread in the needle.

Leaving the basting stitches in position, gently steam press the finished embroidery on the wrong side.

MOUNTING

You can use either of the methods described on page 9 to mount your finished embroidery. To achieve a smooth finish, you may find that it is helpful to secure the fabric to one edge of the board with pins, working from the centre point out to both corners, and then repeat for the opposite side, to make sure that the fabric is even and taut. Secure with tape or lacing, and then repeat for the remaining sides.

If you are setting the mounted fabric in the frame yourself, use rustproof pins to secure the backing board, and seal the back of the picture with broad tape, to ensure that dust cannot enter the frame.

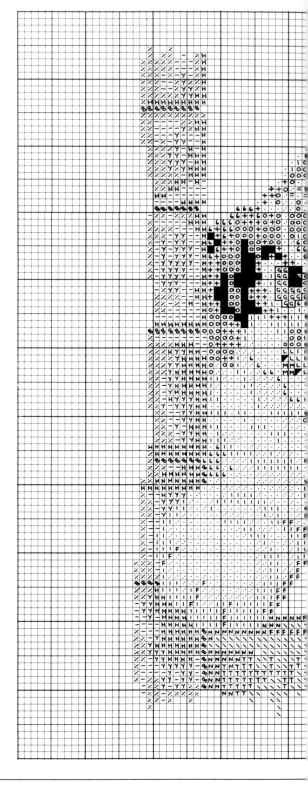

FRAMED PICTURE ▲	DMC	ANCHOR	MADEIRA
■ Black	310	403	Black
G Khaki	733	280	1611
• White	White	2	White
X Dark mahogany brown	300	352	2304
L Peach	353	8	0304
M Medium peach	352	9	0303
◢ Brick red	355	5968	0401
‖ Medium mahogany brown	301	370	2306
Z Light old gold	676	891	2208
6 Dark pewter grey	535	401	1809

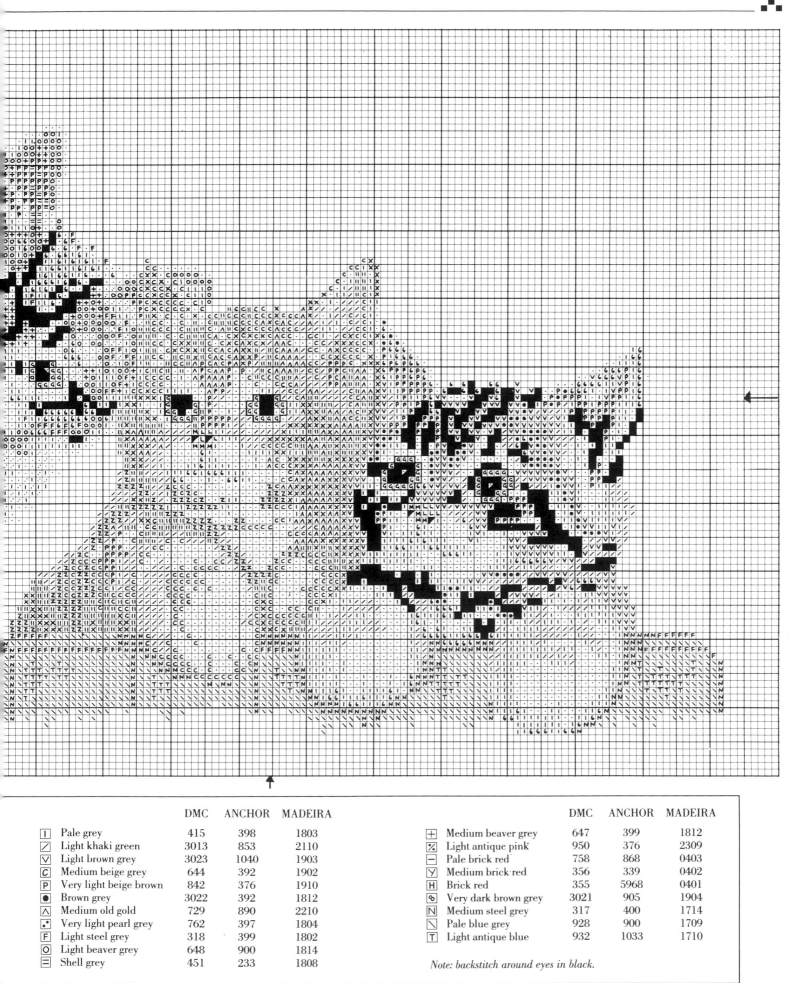

	DMC	ANCHOR	MADEIRA			DMC	ANCHOR	MADEIRA
I Pale grey	415	398	1803		+ Medium beaver grey	647	399	1812
⁄ Light khaki green	3013	853	2110		% Light antique pink	950	376	2309
V Light brown grey	3023	1040	1903		− Pale brick red	758	868	0403
C Medium beige grey	644	392	1902		Y Medium brick red	356	339	0402
P Very light beige brown	842	376	1910		H Brick red	355	5968	0401
● Brown grey	3022	392	1812		☙ Very dark brown grey	3021	905	1904
∧ Medium old gold	729	890	2210		N Medium steel grey	317	400	1714
⋅ Very light pearl grey	762	397	1804		＼ Pale blue grey	928	900	1709
F Light steel grey	318	399	1802		T Light antique blue	932	1033	1710
O Light beaver grey	648	900	1814					
═ Shell grey	451	233	1808		*Note: backstitch around eyes in black.*			

Samplers for Children

A new baby! Record the excitement, laughter, joy and celebration in a lovingly-stitched birth sampler. In the first design, two slender storks, encircled by a heart, hold a bouquet over the baby's name and date of birth. This sampler is worked in soft shades – pastel colours to echo those tender feelings a new baby rouses in every heart.

The motif sampler makes full use of a paint-box palette and appealing images to create a bright, bold design. Motifs carefully chosen for their childhood charm surround the baby's name and birthdate. The delightful duck and teddy are stitched separately as matching pictures.

SAMPLERS FOR CHILDREN

YOU WILL NEED

For each of the designs – Stork, Motif, Duck and Teddy – you will need the following, plus the individual requirements specified below:

Stranded embroidery cotton in the colours given in the appropriate panel
No24 tapestry needle
Strong thread, for lacing across the back
Cardboard, for mounting, sufficient to fit into the frame recess
Frame of your choice

For the *Stork* sampler, with a design area measuring 16cm × 20cm (6¼in × 8in), or 89 stitches by 114 stitches, here in a frame measuring 25cm × 30cm (10in × 12in):

26cm × 30cm (10¼in × 12in) of white, 14-count Aida fabric

For the *Motif* sampler, with a design area measuring 20cm × 15cm (8in × 6in), or 112 stitches by 86 stitches, here in a frame measuring 32cm × 27.5cm (12¾in × 11in):

30cm × 25cm (12in × 10in) of white, 14-count Aida fabric

For the *Duck* picture, with a design area measuring 6.5cm × 6cm (2½in × 2¼in), or 36 stitches by 35 stitches, here in a frame measuring 17cm (6¾in) square:

13cm × 12cm (5in × 4½in) of white, 14-count Aida fabric

For the *Teddy* picture, with a design area measuring 7cm × 6.5cm (2¾in × 2½in), or 38 stitches by 36 stitches, here in a frame measuring 17cm (6¾in) square:

14cm × 13cm (5½in × 5in) of white, 14-count Aida fabric

THE EMBROIDERY

In each case, prepare the fabric and stretch it in a frame (see page 7). Following the appropriate chart, start at the centre of the design, using two strands of cotton in the needle. Work each stitch over one block of fabric in each direction. Make sure that all top crosses run in the same direction and that each row is worked into the same holes as the top or bottom of the row before, so that you do not leave a space between rows.

For the Stork sampler, embroider the leaf stems with two strands of green cotton and the bow with two strands of dark pink cotton. Outline the heart and the storks, and embroider the feet, name and date with one strand of dark brown cotton. If you are making the sampler for a boy, you might choose to embroider the flowers in blue rather than pink.

For the Motif sampler and pictures, the motifs are outlined in backstitch with one strand of dark grey cotton, and the date and ladybird legs are worked with two strands of dark grey. The duck's eye is a single french knot in dark grey cotton.

MAKING UP

Gently steam press the finished embroideries on the wrong side and mount them as explained on page 9. When choosing the mounts and frames, consider the colour scheme of the room, as the set of pictures will make a striking and attractive feature.

STORK ▶		DMC	ANCHOR	MADEIRA
+	Cream	746	275	0101
o	Light pink	3689	66	0606
s	Dark pink	3688	68	0605
‡	Green	368	214	1310
<	Light brown	842	376	1910
=	Dark brown	840	679	1912

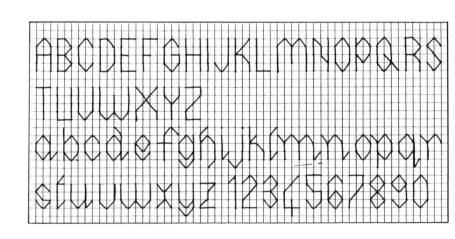

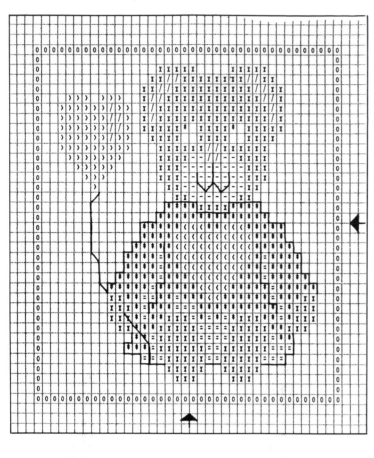

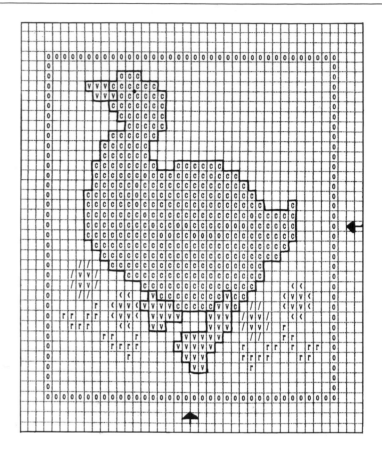

TEDDY ▲		DMC	ANCHOR	MADEIRA
╱	Light pink	3689	66	0606
⟨	Dark pink	3688	68	0605
⟩	Dark mauve	208	111	0804
–	Gold	676	887	2208
‡	Light blue	800	128	0908
=	Dark blue	799	130	0910
x	Brown	434	365	2009
o	Light grey	415	398	1803
	Dark grey*	414	399	1801

Note: dark grey* is used for backstitch outline.

DUCK ▲		DMC	ANCHOR	MADEIRA
c	Cream	746	275	0101
╱	Light pink	3689	66	0606
⟨	Dark pink	3688	68	0605
v	Yellow	3078	292	0102
r	Green	3348	264	1409
o	Light grey	415	398	1803
	Dark grey*	414	399	1801

Note: dark blue (see Motif Sampler) used for eye only; dark grey* is used for backstitch.

MOTIF SAMPLER ▶		DMC	ANCHOR	MADEIRA
c	Cream	746	275	0101
╱	Light pink	3689	66	0606
⟨	Dark pink	3688	68	0605
╲	Light mauve	210	109	0803
⟩	Dark mauve	208	111	0804
+	Crimson	309	42	0510
v	Yellow	3078	292	0102
–	Gold	676	887	2208
‡	Light blue	800	128	0908
=	Dark blue	799	130	0910
r	Green	3348	264	1409
x	Brown	434	365	2009
o	Light grey	415	398	1803
	Dark grey*	414	399	1801

Note: dark grey* is used for backstitch outline.

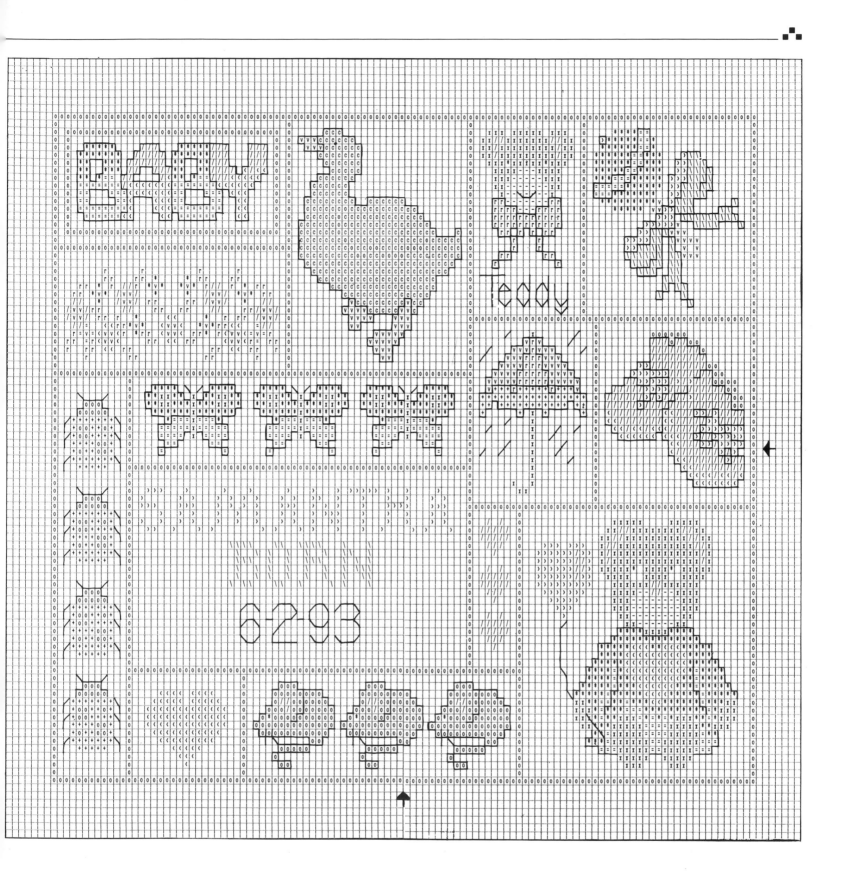

Teddy Pictures

These delightful miniature pictures
will make an attractive addition
to your home, whether displayed
singly or together.
Either of the designs would make a
lovely gift to welcome a new baby.

TEDDY PICTURES

For the Balloon Bear picture, measuring
18cm × 13cm (7¼in × 5in), framed:

23cm (9in) square of ecru, 18-count
Ainring Aida fabric
Stranded embroidery cotton in the colours
given in the appropriate panel
No26 tapestry needle
Oval brass frame (for suppliers, see page 144)

For the Reading Bears picture, measuring
15cm (6in) in diameter, framed:

23cm (9in) square of ecru, 18-count
Ainring Aida fabric
Stranded embroidery cotton in the colours
given in the appropriate panel
No26 tapestry needle
Round brass frame (for suppliers, see page 144)

•

THE EMBROIDERY

Both designs are stitched in the same way and on
the same type of fabric. If you wish to embroider
them both, you may be able to economize on fabric
by using one large piece, remembering to allow
sufficient space between the pictures.

Prepare the fabric, marking the centre lines of
(each) design with basting stitches, and mount it in
a hoop, following the instructions on page 6. Referring to the appropriate chart, complete the cross
stitching, starting at the centre and using two
strands in the needle throughout. Embroider the
main areas first, and then finish with the backstitching, this time using one strand of thread in the
needle. Steam press on the wrong side.

It is a good idea to leave the basting stitches in
at this stage, as they will prove useful in helping to
centre your design in the frame.

FRAMING A PICTURE

Each picture is framed in the same way. Gently
remove all parts of the frame. Place the card template over the chart and mark the centre both ways,
using a soft pencil. Lay the embroidery face down
with the card on top, matching basting stitches and
lines, and draw around the card with a pencil.

Working freehand, draw a second line about 4cm
(1½in) outside, and cut along this outer line.

With double sewing thread in the needle, make a
line of running stitches about 2cm (¾in) in from the
raw edge, close to the marked line. Place the card on
the wrong side and pull up the thread, spacing the
gathers evenly, and making sure the fabric grain is
straight. Secure the thread firmly. Add pieces of
masking tape over the edges of the fabric for extra
strength. Finish the assembly, following the manufacturer's instructions.

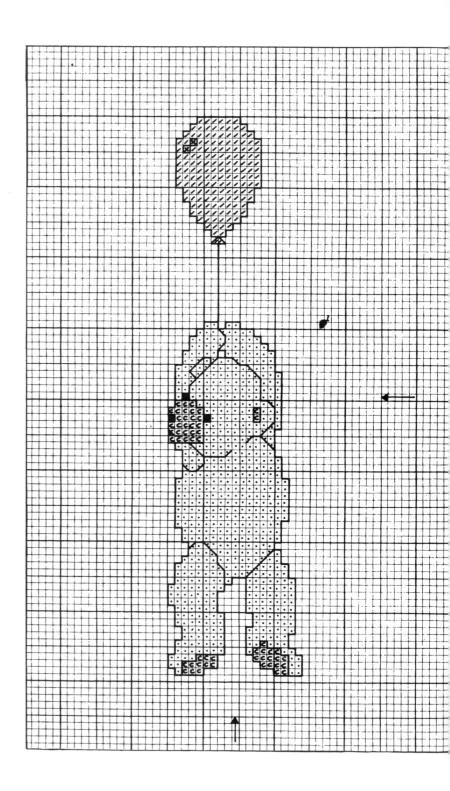

READING BEARS ▲	DMC	ANCHOR	MADEIRA
☐ White	White	2	White
• Dark peach	351	10	0214
╱ Topaz	725	306	0108
L Light old gold	676	891	2208
o Dark old gold	680	901	2210
⊙ Medium blue	826	161	1012
‖ Very light brown	435	365	2010
● Medium brown	433	371	2008
Very dark beaver*	844	401	1810
■ Black	310	403	Black

Note: black used for backstitch eyes, other outlines very dark beaver*.

BALLOON BEAR ◄	DMC	ANCHOR	MADEIRA
x White	White	2	White
╱ Medium blue	826	161	1012
c Very light tan	738	942	2013
• Light brown	434	309	2009
Very dark beaver*	844	401	1810
■ Black	310	403	Black

Note: very dark beaver* used for backstitch outlines.

Country Mice

These two delightful studies of mice – one sheltering under toadstools and one surrounded by poppies – would be ideal for a child's bedroom, but would also look charming in a bathroom or hallway.

COUNTRY MICE

YOU WILL NEED

For either the *Toadstool Mouse* or the *Poppy Mouse*
picture, each set in a frame measuring
23cm × 18cm (9in × 7in), with an oval cut-out
measuring 19cm × 14cm (7½ × 5½in):

*30cm × 27.5cm (12in × 11in) of white,
14-count Aida fabric
Stranded embroidery cotton in the colours
given in the panel*

*No24 tapestry needle
One small dark brown or black bead (optional)
Picture frame
Picture mount to fit the frame, with an oval aperture
as specified above
Firm card, to fit the frame
Lightweight synthetic batting, the same size
as the card
Strong thread, for mounting
Glue stick*

*NOTE One skein of each colour listed is
sufficient for both pictures.*

THE EMBROIDERY

Prepare the fabric as described on page 6; find the centre either by folding the fabric in half and then in half again, and lightly pressing the folded corner, or by marking the horizontal and vertical centre lines with basting stitches in a light-coloured thread. Mount the fabric in a frame (see page 7) and count out from the centre to start the design at an appropriate point.

Following the chart, complete all the cross stitching first, using two strands of thread in the needle. Finish with the eye of the mouse, which is formed by one dark brown cross stitch. If you choose, you may add a small bead to the eye, which will bring it to life.

MOUNTING AND FRAMING

Remove the finished embroidery from the frame and wash if necessary, then press lightly on the wrong side, using a steam iron. Spread glue evenly on one side of the firm card, and lightly press the batting to the surface. Lace the embroidery over the padded surface (see page 9), using the basting stitches (if any) to check that the embroidery is centred over the card. Remove basting stitches, place the mounted embroidery in the frame, behind the oval mount, and assemble the frame according to the manufacturer's instructions.

COUNTRY MICE		ANCHOR	DMC	MADEIRA
•	White	2	Blanc	White
–	Cream	300	745	111
C	Light green	238	703	1307
O	Medium green	258	904	1413
●	Dark green	245	986	1405
2	Bright red	335	606	209
3	Medium red	19	817	212
4	Dark red	20	498	513
I	Beige	381	938	2005
H	Light brown	374	420	2104
■	Dark brown	380	839	1913

A Picture for Baby

This charming picture would certainly win the heart of anyone with a newborn baby. Traditionalists will no doubt sew the letters in blue for a boy, or pink for a girl.

A PICTURE FOR BABY

YOU WILL NEED

For the picture, measuring 50cm × 24cm (20in × 9½), unframed:

*58.5cm × 31.5cm (23in × 12½in) of white,
14-count Aida fabric
Stranded embroidery cotton in the colours given
in the panel; two skeins of tan are required, and
three of either baby blue or pale dusty rose
50cm × 24cm (20in × 9½in) of firm cardboard,
for a mount
50cm × 24cm (20in × 9½in) of iron-on
interfacing (optional – see Mounting the picture)
No24 tapestry needle
Picture frame of your choice*

THE EMBROIDERY

Prepare the fabric, marking the centre lines of the design with basting stitches, and mount it in a frame, following the instructions on page 7. Referring to the chart, complete the cross stitching, using three strands in the needle throughout. Embroider the main areas first, and then finish with the backstitching, this time using two strands of thread in the needle. If necessary, steam press on the wrong side.

It is a good idea to leave the basting stitches in at this stage, as they will prove useful in helping to centre your design on the mount.

MOUNTING THE PICTURE

Take care that your working surface is absolutely clean and dry. If you wish to use an iron-on interfacing, to help to avoid wrinkles, iron this to the back of the embroidery, following the same procedure as for the cards on page 48. If you are not using interfacing, leave the basting stitches in place and remove them after mounting.

Mount your picture on the firm cardboard, following the instructions given for heavier fabrics. Mark the centre of the board at the top, bottom and sides, and match centre marks for accurate alignment.

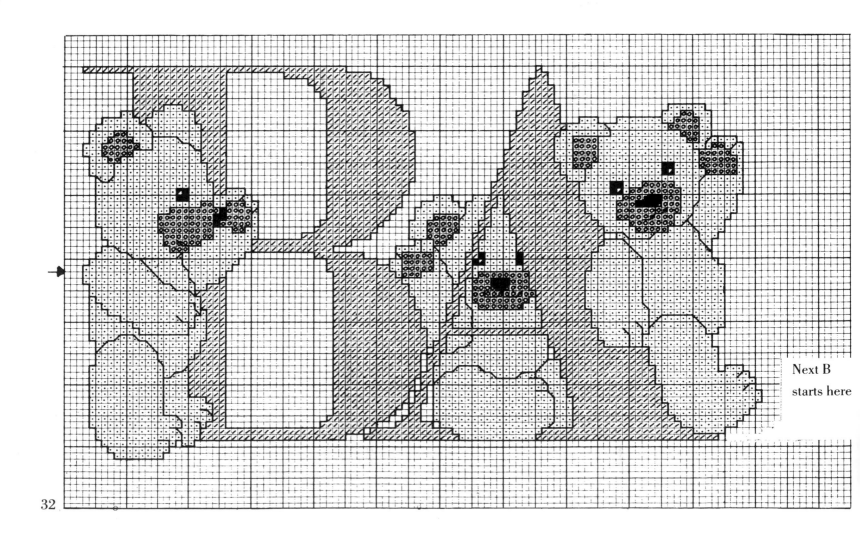

Next B
starts here

PICTURE FOR BABY	DMC	ANCHOR	MADEIRA
△ White	White	2	White
╱ Baby blue	3325	159	1002
Dark baby blue*	322	978	1004
╱ Pale dusty rose	963	48	0608
Dark dusty rose*	961	40	0610
o Pale golden wheat	3047	886	2205
• Tan	436	363	2011
Medium brown*	433	371	2008
■ Black	310	403	Black

Note: outline pale golden wheat with medium brown, baby blue with dark baby blue* or pale dusty rose with dark dusty rose* (starred colours are used for backstitching only); use either baby blues (for a boy) or dusty pinks (for a girl); two skeins needed of tan, and three of either baby blue or pale dusty rose.*

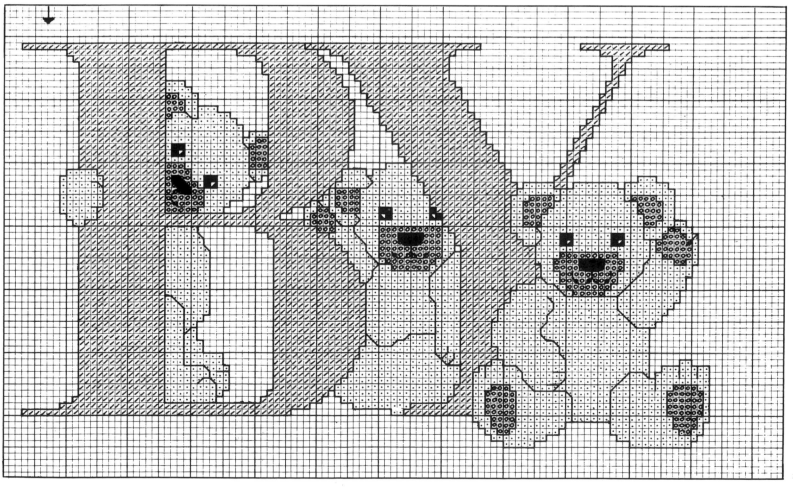

Wildlife Studies

Make them as five separate cards to delight your family and friends, or combine them into a single charming picture – whichever you choose, this set of wildlife studies will prove enjoyable to stitch. The individual designs are relatively simple and could prove a pleasant exercise for a child learning embroidery.

WILDLIFE STUDIES

YOU WILL NEED

For the picture, set in a frame with a centre measuring 22.5cm × 17.5cm (9in × 7in):

35cm × 30cm (14in × 12in) of antique white, 14-count Aida fabric
Stranded embroidery cotton in the colours given in the panel
No26 tapestry needle
Picture frame, as specified above
Firm card, to fit the frame
Lightweight synthetic batting, the same size as the card
Strong thread, for mounting
Glue stick

For each card:

15cm × 12.5cm (6in × 5in) of antique white, 14-count Aida fabric
Stranded embroidery cotton in the colours given in the panel
No26 tapestry needle
Card with an aperture measuring 10cm × 7.5cm (4in × 3in), designed for embroidery (for suppliers, see page 148)

●

THE EMBROIDERY

Prepare the fabric as described on page 6; find the centre either by folding the fabric in half and then in half again, and lightly pressing the folded corner, or by marking the horizontal and vertical centre lines with basting stitches in a light-coloured thread. If you are making the picture, mount the fabric in a frame (see page 7); individual designs can be stitched without a frame.

Count out from the centre to start at an appropriate point. Following the chart, complete the cross stitching first, using two strands of thread in the needle. Finish with the backstitched details, again using two strands of thread in the needle. Be careful not to take dark threads across the back of the work in such a way that they show through on to the right side of the embroidery. Remove the finished embroidery from the frame, if used, and wash if necessary, then press lightly on the wrong side, using a steam iron.

MOUNTING THE PICTURE

Spread glue evenly on one side of the firm card, and lightly press the batting to the surface. Lace the embroidery over the padded surface (see page 9), using the basting stitches (if any) to check that the embroidery is centred over the card. Remove basting stitches, place the mounted embroidery in the frame, and assemble the frame according to the manufacturer's instructions.

THE CARDS

For each card, trim the embroidery to measure about 12mm (½in) larger all around than the size of the card window. Remove basting stitches. Position the embroidery behind the window; open out the self-adhesive mount; fold the card, and press firmly to secure it. Some cards require a dab of glue to ensure a secure and neat finish.

WILDLIFE STUDIES ▶	ANCHOR	DMC	MADEIRA
• White	1	Blanc	White
– Silver grey	397	453	1807
I Medium grey	399	318	1802
X Dark grey	400	317	1714
■ Black	403	310	Black
C Light warm brown	369	435	2010
O Medium warm brown	370	433	2008
+ Dark warm brown	371	739	2303
● Dark brown	905	3781	2106
V Light grass green	226	702	1306
∧ Medium grass green	228	700	1304

Note: backstitch ears of squirrel, badger, rabbit and pole cat in black, and badger's eye in white.

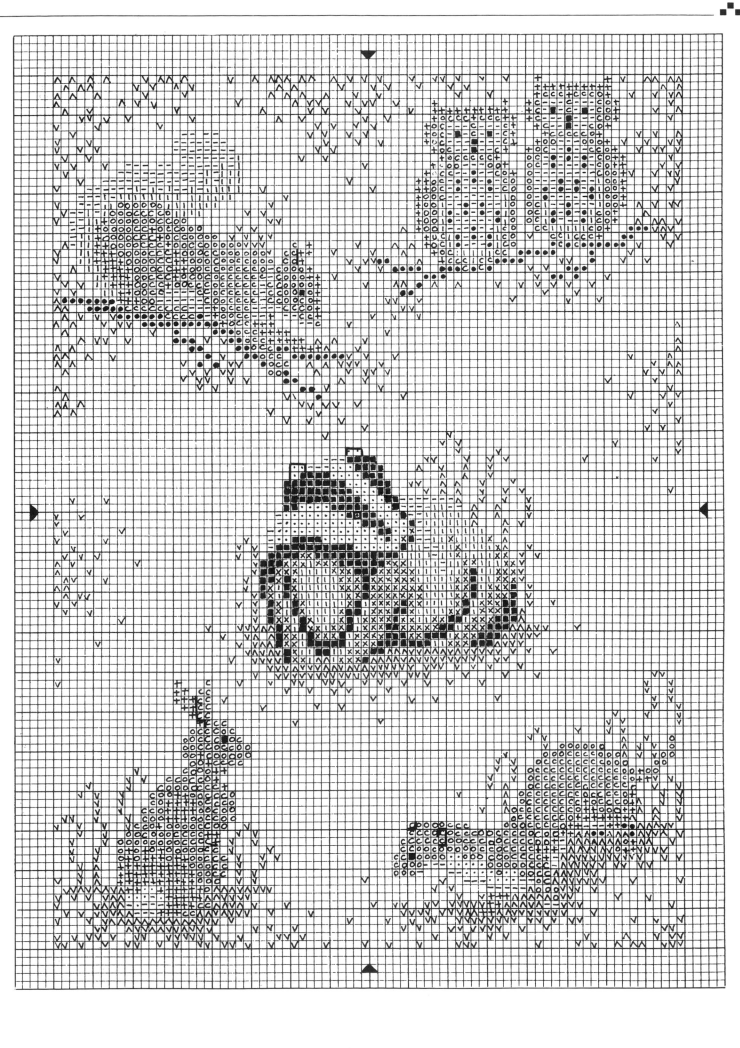

SPECIAL OCCASIONS

A cross stitched memento is a charming way to celebrate a special occasion, whether it is Christmas, a birthday, or the arrival of a new member of the family. The Christmas stocking seen here would be treasured and brought out year after year, while the quilted wall hanging on page 62 would set the scene for many a Christmas gathering.

CHRISTMAS STOCKING

YOU WILL NEED

For the Christmas stocking, measuring
25cm × 18cm (10in × 7¼in) overall:

*Two 30cm (12in) squares of navy, 14-count
Aida fabric
1.1m (1¼yd) of red bias binding
Stranded embroidery cotton in the colours given
in the panel
Metallic threads in gold and silver
Two 30cm (12in) squares of lightweight synthetic
batting (optional)
Two 30cm (12in) squares of lining fabric, in navy
or a contrast colour (optional)
Matching red sewing thread
No24 tapestry needle*

*NOTE The stocking seen here is unlined, but if you
wish to make a lined and padded version, for
greater durability – and to help to conceal the
shapes of the contents – you will require the
optional batting and lining listed above.*

•

THE EMBROIDERY

Prepare the fabric, marking the centre lines of the
design with basting stitches, and mount it in a hoop
or frame, following the instructions on page 7.
Referring to the chart, complete the cross stitching,
starting at the centre and using three strands in the
needle when working with stranded cotton and two
strands when using the metallic thread. Embroider
the main areas first, and then finish with the backstitching, using two strands of cotton in the needle.
Remove basting stitches and, if necessary, steam
press on the wrong side.

MAKING UP THE STOCKING

Trace the template for the stocking outline on tracing
paper, marking the position of the arrows. It is not
necessary to cut out the shape at this stage, simply
pin the tracing paper to the embroidery fabric,
making sure that the embroidery falls in the correct
position, or use strips of masking tape to hold it in
place. Cut out the shape, then cut out a mirror image
shape from the fabric that is not embroidered.
  If you wish to make a hanging loop for the stocking,

take a short length of binding – approximately 5cm
(2in). Bring the folded edges together and slipstitch.
Set the strip to one side.
  Place the two pieces of fabric with wrong sides
together and baste. Taking a 12mm (½in) seam
allowance, machine around the stocking, leaving the
top edge open. Trim the seam neatly to 6mm (¼in)
from the stitching line. Remove the basting stitches.
  Bind around the trimmed seam to neaten it: open
out the turning on one edge of the bias binding and
pin it in position on the right side of the fabric,
matching the fold to the seamline. Fold over the cut
end and overlap the starting point by 12mm (½in).
Baste and machine stitch along the seamline then
bring the binding over the raw edge and hem neatly,
using masking thread. Alternatively, simple place
the binding over the edge, and machine stitch
through all layers, close to the folded edge. If you are
adding a hanging loop, take the prepared strip of
binding and fold it in two. Position the loop at the top
of the back seam of the stocking, with the raw edges
level with the raw edge of the stocking top. Bind
around the top of the stocking, catching the loop in
with the binding.

LINED VERSION

If you are making a padded and lined version, use
the template to cut out a pair of shapes each from the
batting and lining fabrics. Before making up the
stocking as described above, place a fabric, batting
and lining shape together, with the batting in the
middle of the sandwich and the lining and fabric
layers right side outwards. Pin and baste together.
Repeat for the other half of the stocking, then
proceed to make up the stocking as described above,
but trim the batting right back to the seamline before
adding the binding.

CHRISTMAS ▶ STOCKING		ANCHOR	DMC	MADEIRA
∴	White	2	White	White
o	Medium violet	98	553	0712
‖	Christmas red	47	321	0510
●	Garnet red	43	815	0513
·	Pale golden wheat	886	3047	2205
c	Bright canary	297	973	0105
v	Kelly green	226	702	1306
∕	Tan	363	436	2011
∧	Medium brown	371	433	2008
■	Black	403	310	Black
H	Silver thread			
=	Gold thread			

Note: black used for backstitched mouth.

The New Arrival

The arrival of a new addition to the family is always a cause for great joy – and the decoration of nursery items and clothing is a lovely and lasting way of celebrating this special occasion. Several baby motifs are here used in different ways; they could also be applied to baby linens, used as tiny nursery pictures or to decorate other items of clothing and the like.

THE NEW ARRIVAL

YOU WILL NEED

For the *Teddy Bear* card, with an oval aperture measuring 6.5cm × 8cm (2½in × 3¼in):

*10cm × 15cm (4in × 6in) of white, 18-count
Aida fabric
Ribbon trim (optional)
Stranded embroidery cotton in the colours given
in the appropriate panel
No26 tapestry needle
Purchased card, for suppliers see page 144*

For the baby vest and socks:

*Approximately 20cm × 15cm (8in × 6in) of
waste canvas
Stranded embroidery cotton in the colours given
in the appropriate panel
No24 tapestry needle
Purchased vest and socks, or other items
of clothing*

For the baby bib:

*Stranded embroidery cotton in the colours given
in the appropriate panel
No24 tapestry needle
Purchased bib, for suppliers see page 144*

•

THE EMBROIDERY

For the card, prepare the fabric (see page 6) and either set it in a hoop or stitch with it in the hand. Use one strand of thread in the needle throughout, for cross stitches and backstitching.

Trim the finished embroidery to measure slightly larger all round than the card window, then centre it behind the window, using the basting stitches as guidelines. Make light pencil marks on the back of the embroidery and the back of the window, to act as registration marks. Remove the basting stitches, then replace the card in the window. Use double-sided tape to secure the card in position, then press the backing down firmly. Attach the ribbon trim, if desired, with either a dab of fabric glue or a piece of double-sided tape.

For the vest and socks, prepare the items by basting waste canvas pieces in position over the design areas and stitch over the canvas.

Use two strands of embroidery cotton in the needle for cross stitches and one for backstitching. When you have finished, remove the basting stitches. Lightly dampen the canvas and then, using tweezers, slowly and gently pull out the canvas threads, one at a time.

For the baby bib, also use two strands for cross stitches and one for backstitching.

TEDDY BEAR ▶		DMC	ANCHOR	MADEIRA
B	Pale blue	3752	343	1710
O	Pale shell pink	3713	48	0502
S	Pale yellow	745	300	0111
•	White	White	2	White
■	Dark golden brown	610	889	2119
X	Light tan	738	361	2013
V	Very light tan	739	366	2014
T	Golden tan	437	362	2012

Note: use dark golden brown for all backstitching.

ROCKING HORSE ▶		DMC	ANCHOR	MADEIRA
B	Pale blue	3752	343	1710
O	Pale shell pink	3713	48	0502
P	Medium salmon pink	761	8	0404
■	Dark golden brown*	610	889	2119
Y	Medium yellow	744	301	0112

Note: use dark golden brown (not used for cross stitching) for all backstitching and to make a french knot for the eye.*

CHICK ▶		DMC	ANCHOR	MADEIRA
B	Pale blue	3752	343	1710
S	Pale yellow	745	300	0111
■	Dark golden brown*	610	889	2119
Y	Medium yellow	744	301	0112

Note: use dark golden brown (not used for cross stitching) for all backstitching and to make a french knot for the eye.*

PRAM ▶		DMC	ANCHOR	MADEIRA
B	Pale blue	3752	343	1710
O	Pale shell pink	3713	48	0502
P	Medium salmon pink	761	8	0404
■	Dark golden brown	610	889	2119
X	Light tan	738	361	2013
V	Very light tan	739	361	2014
T	Golden tan	437	362	2012

Note: use dark golden brown for all backstitching

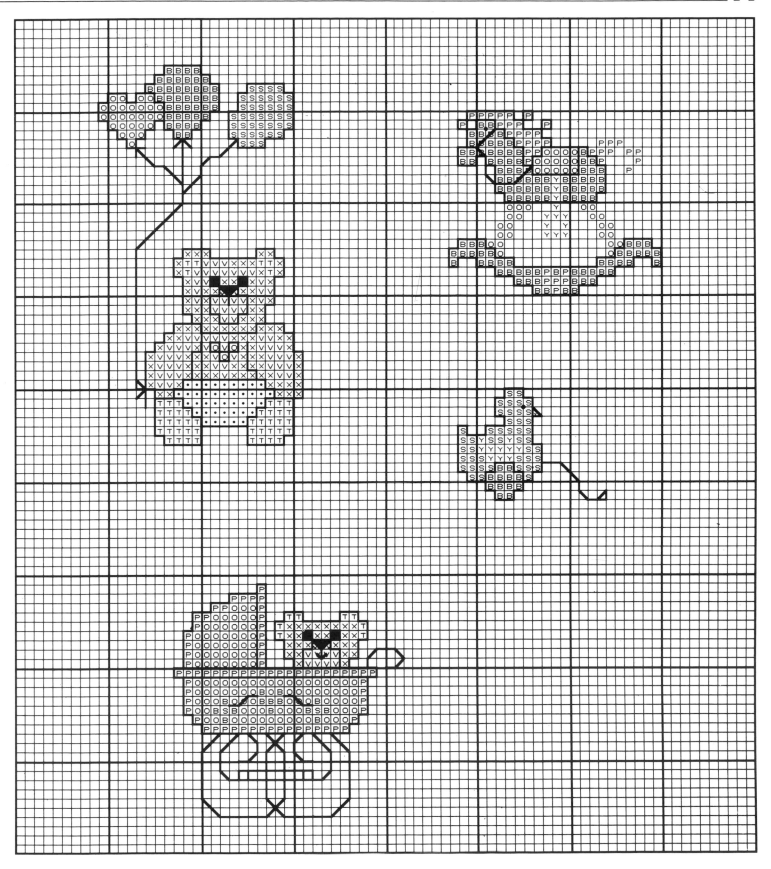

Teddy Bear Cards

Whichever teddy you choose to
embroider he will be a pleasure to
make and a way of showing that the
recipient is special.

TEDDY BEAR CARDS

YOU WILL NEED

For each card, measuring 15.5cm × 11cm
(6¼in × 4in):

*19cm × 15cm (7½in × 6in) of white, 22-count
Hardanger fabric
Stranded embroidery cotton in the colours given in
the appropriate panel
No26 tapestry needle
Double-sided adhesive tape
Card mount (for suppliers, see page 144),
as appropriate:
Christmas Bear card – holly green with round
inner frame, 8cm (3in) in diameter
Birthday Bear card – pale blue with round
inner frame 8cm (3in) in diameter
Valentine Bear card – Christmas red with oval
inner frame, 10.5cm × 8cm (4½in × 3in)
Iron-on interfacing (optional – see Making up the
cards) – 12mm larger all-round than the size of
the inner frame of the chosen card*

•

THE EMBROIDERY

All three cards are stitched in the same way and
on the same type of fabric.

Note that it is particularly important with
embroidered cards to avoid excessive overstitching
on the back, as this would cause unsightly lumps
to show through on the right side.

Prepare the fabric, marking the centre lines of
each design with basting stitches, and mount it in
a small hoop, following the instructions on page 6.
Referring to the appropriate chart, complete the
cross stitching, using a single strand in the needle
throughout. Embroider the main areas first, and
then finish with the backstitching. If necessary,
steam press on the wrong side.

It is a good idea to leave the basting stitches in
at this stage, as they will prove useful in helping to
centre your design in the card window.

MAKING UP THE CARDS

It is not strictly necessary to use iron-on interfacing,
but it helps to avoid wrinkles. If you are using interfacing, place it on the back of the embroidery; use a
pencil to mark the basting/registration points on
the interfacing and outer edge of the embroidery.

Remove basting stitches and iron the interfacing in
place, aligning marks.

Trim the embroidery to about 12mm (½in) larger
than the cut-out window, and then, making sure that
the motif is placed in the middle by measuring an
equal distance at each side of the marks, position the
embroidery behind the window. Use double-sided
tape to fix the embroidery into the card, then press
the backing down firmly.

BIRTHDAY ▼		DMC	ANCHOR	MADEIRA
□	White	White	2	White
‖	Medium pink	899	27	0505
x	Deep rose	309	42	0507
c	Delft blue	809	130	0909
	Royal blue*	797	132	0912
I	Light tan	738	942	2013
•	Light brown	434	309	2009
	Very dark coffee*	898	360	2006
■	Black	310	403	Black

Note: black used to backstitch around the mouth, very dark coffee for
bear, royal blue* (starred colours are used for bks only) for ribbon.*

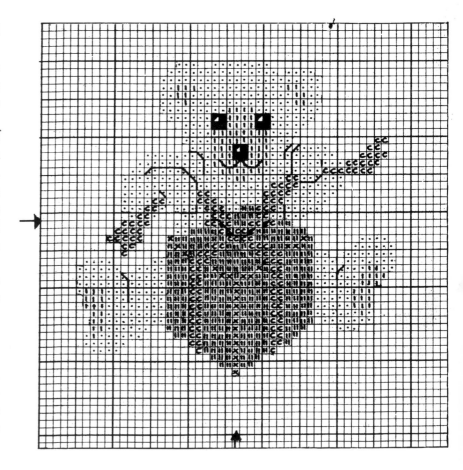

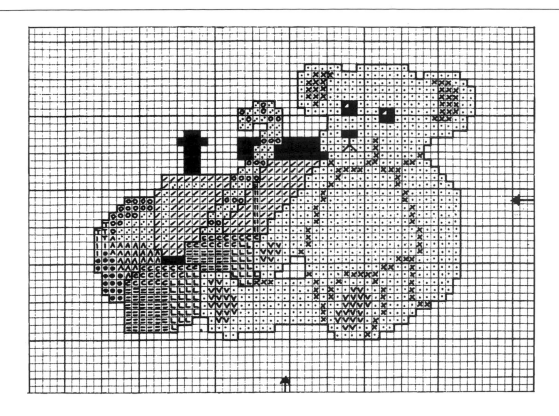

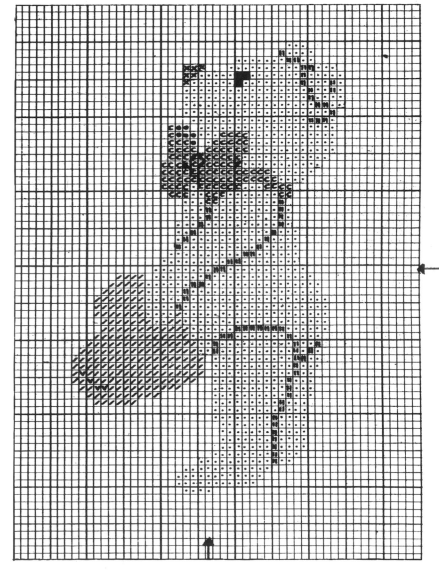

CHRISTMAS ▲		DMC	ANCHOR	MADEIRA
∴	White	White	2	White
c	Pink	3326	26	0504
o	Bright red	666	46	0210
L	Dark lavender	208	110	0804
●	Light pumpkin	970	316	0204
X	Medium tangerine	741	304	0201
·	Dark yellow	743	297	0113
Λ	Medium bright blue	996	433	1103
=	Delft blue	809	130	0909
T	Dark blue	825	162	1011
I	Light emerald	912	209	1212
/	Light green	989	256	1401
II	Dark green	987	245	1403
V	Medium gold brown	976	309	2302
	Very dark grey*	844	401	1810
■	Black	310	403	Black

Note: very dark grey* used for backstitch outlines, and black for mouth.

VALENTINE ▶		DMC	ANCHOR	MADEIRA
V	White	White	2	White
/	Red	349	13	0212
c	Medium baby blue	334	161	1003
●	Light navy	312	147	1005
	Medium navy*	311	148	1006
·	Medium old gold	729	907	2209
II	Dark topaz brown	781	308	2213
X	Dark coffee	801	357	2007
■	Black	310	403	Black

Note: medium navy* used for backstitched ribbon.

Cards for Cat Lovers

Small greetings cards, each containing a tiny embroidery, are easy to make. Here are three lovely caricature cat designs, one for Christmas, one to offer congratulations (perhaps for an 18th or 21st birthday, an engagement or an anniversary) and a Valentine's Day card.

GREETINGS CARDS

YOU WILL NEED

For each card, measuring 15.5cm × 11cm
(6¼in × 14⅜in):

*19cm × 15cm (7½in × 6in) of white, 22-count
Hardanger fabric
Stranded embroidery cotton in the colours
given in the appropriate panel
No 26 tapestry needle
Double-sided adhesive tape
Iron-on interfacing (optional, see Making up the
cards) – 12mm (½in) larger all around than the
size of the inner frame of your chosen card.
Card mount (for suppliers, see page 144),
as appropriate:
Cat's Christmas – holly green with a
rectangular cut-out
Champagne Charlies – pale blue with an
oval cut-out
Valentine's Day – Christmas red with an
oval cut-out*

•

THE EMBROIDERY

Each of these designs is stitched in the same way
and on the same type of fabric. If you wish to
embroider all three, you may be able to economize
on fabric by using one large piece, remembering to
allow sufficient space between each design.

Note that it is particularly important with
embroidered cards to avoid excessive overstitching
on the back, as this would cause unsightly lumps
to show through on the right side.

Prepare the fabric, marking the centre lines of
each design with basting stitches, and mount it in
a small hoop, following the instructions on page 6.
Referring to the appropriate chart, complete the
cross stitching, using a single strand in the needle
throughout. Embroider the main areas first, and
then finish with the backstitching. If necessary,
steam press on the wrong side.

It is a good idea to leave the basting stitches in
at this stage, as they will prove useful in helping to
centre your design in the card window.

MAKING UP THE CARDS

It is not strictly necessary to use iron-on interfacing,
but it helps to avoid wrinkles. If you are using
interfacing, place it on the back of the embroidery;
use a pencil to mark the basting/registration points
on the interfacing and outer edge of the embroidery.
Remove basting stitches and iron the interfacing in
place, aligning marks.

Trim the embroidery to about 12mm (½in) larger
than the cut-out window, and then, making sure
that the motif is placed in the middle by measuring an equal distance at each side of the marks,
position the embroidery behind the window. Use
double-sided tape to fix the embroidery into the
card, then press the backing down firmly.

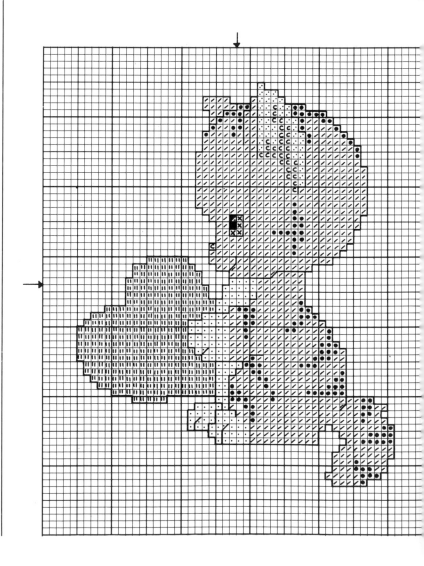

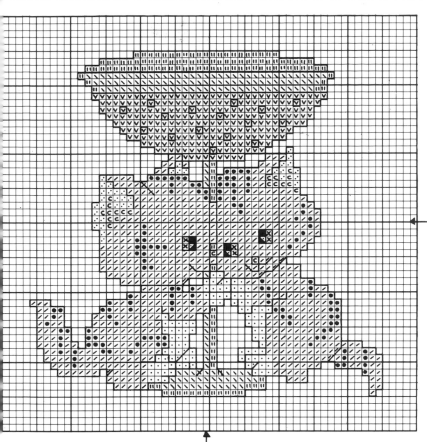

CAT'S CHRISTMAS ▼		DMC	ANCHOR	MADEIRA
C	Coral	351	10	0214
∴	Peach	353	9	0304
●	Medium tangerine	741	314	0201
╱	Primrose yellow	744	301	0112
•	White	White	2	White
Z	Silver thread			
‖	Red	666	46	0210
V	Christmas green	700	228	1305
⊠	Gold thread			
═	Apple green	702	239	1306
L	Old gold	725	306	0108
∧	Mauve	333	111	0903

Note: bks outlines in black.

CHAMPAGNE CHARLIES ▲

		DMC	ANCHOR	MADEIRA
V	Light old gold	676	891	2208
N	Very light pearl grey	762	397	1804
‖	Pale grey	415	398	1803
╱	Primrose yellow	744	301	0112
●	Medium tangerine	741	314	0201
⊠	Light yellowy green	3348	264	1409
•	White	White	2	White
C	Coral	351	10	0214
∴	Peach	353	9	0304
■	Black	310	403	Black

VALENTINE'S DAY ◄

		DMC	ANCHOR	MADEIRA
•	White	White	2	White
⊠	Light yellowy green	3348	264	1409
‖	Red	666	46	0210
╱	Primrose yellow	744	301	0112
●	Medium tangerine	741	314	0201
C	Coral	351	10	0214
∴	Peach	353	9	0304
■	Black	310	403	Black

Antique Bears

Teddy bears never seem to lose their popularity – either in their own right, or as motifs for embroiderers – and justifiably so. This charming trio is stitched in muted shades to give them that well-loved, faded look common to bears; they would make delightful gifts, or you might just stitch them for yourself!

ANTIQUE BEARS

For each bear:

*10cm (4in) square of antique white, 18-count
Aida fabric
Stranded embroidery cotton in the colours given
in the appropriate panel
No26 tapestry needle*

For the *Patchwork Bear:*

*A frosted glass bowl, 6.5cm (2¹⁄₂in) in diameter, for
suppliers see page 144*

For the *Garden Bear:*

*An oval porcelain box, in ivory,
7cm × 5cm (2⁷⁄₈in × 2in), for suppliers see page 144*

For the *Heart Bear:*

*A cream card, 8.5cm × 6.5in (3³⁄₈in × 2¹⁄₂in), for
suppliers see page 144*

•

THE EMBROIDERY

For each bear, prepare the fabric, marking the centre each way with a horizontal and vertical line of basting stitches (see page 6). If you are embroidering all three designs, you may find it easier to use one large piece of fabric, dividing the separate areas with basting stitches and then marking the centre of each, as described.

One strand of thread is used throughout for all designs. Work all the cross stitches first, making sure that top stitches all lie in the same direction, and then add the backstitch details.

When you have finished the embroidery, wash the fabric, if necessary, and press it lightly on the wrong side. Leave the basting stitches in position at this stage.

THE EMBROIDERY

For the glass bowl and the oval box, follow the manufacturer's instructions. In each case, use the template provided to mark the shape on the fabric, with the basting stitches still in position to help you to ensure that the design is centred. Trim and remove basting stitches, then insert the embroidery into the lid as directed.

For the card, trim the embroidery to measure about 12mm (¹⁄₂in) larger than the opening, each way, using the basting stitches as a guide to ensure that the design is centred. Remove basting stitches; place the embroidery behind the opening, and seal the card.

PATCHWORK BEAR ▶		DMC	ANCHOR	MADEIRA
■	Very dark brown	3031	905	2003
●	Medium tan	435	369	2010
T	Light tan	347	943	1910
I	Pale golden tan	738	361	2013
•	Very pale golden tan	739	366	2014
P	Medium salmon pink	761	8	0404
U	Light shell pink	3713	48	0502
M	Medium lilac	544	97	0711
B	Medium antique blue	932	920	1710

Note: backstitch body and features in very dark brown.

GARDEN BEAR ▶		DMC	ANCHOR	MADEIRA
	Very dark brown*	3031	905	2003
P	Medium salmon pink	761	8	0404
U	Light shell pink	3713	48	0502
B	Medium antique blue	932	920	1710
▲	Dark golden brown	610	889	2119
X	Light golden brown	612	832	2108
O	Very light golden brown	613	831	2109
—	Pale cream	712	926	2101
⁄	Very pale grey green	524	858	1511
N	Medium grey green	522	860	1513
C	Medium blue	3752	343	1710

Note: backstitch body and features in very dark brown (used for bks only), and the stems of the flowers in medium grey green.*

HEART BEAR ▶		DMC	ANCHOR	MADEIRA
	Very dark brown*	3031	905	2003
P	Medium salmon pink	761	8	0404
U	Light shell pink	3713	48	0502
B	Medium antique blue	932	920	1710
＼	Pale silver grey	762	397	1804
◢	Dark beige brown	839	380	1913
R	Medium beige brown	840	354	1912
S	Light beige brown	841	378	1911
V	Very light beige brown	842	376	1910

Note: backstitch body and features in very dark brown (used for bks only).*

Special Occasion Borders

Scattered through the year are a number of festivals, such as Christmas or Easter, and celebrations, including birthdays or Mother's Day. This selection of borders has been designed with these special occasions in mind. The borders can be used for many different items, from table linen to bookmarks, or you might choose to use individual motifs for placecards, or for small gifts or mementoes.

SPECIAL OCCASION BORDERS

YOU WILL NEED

*14-count Aida Ribband, 5cm (2in) wide, in your
chosen colour
Stranded embroidery cotton in the colours given
No24 tapestry needle
Graph paper and coloured pencils or felt-tip pens
(optional)*

*NOTE: Aida Ribband is available in a number of
colours and widths. The length that you require will
depend on the end use of the embroidered band. The
panel lists all the colours used in the complete range
of borders, so check which shades are used in your
chosen border and buy one skein each of those
particular colours only.*

•

PLANNING THE DESIGN

Start by establishing the desired length of your
border, so that you can then calculate the required
number of repeats for that length. Unless the design
is very long, the easiest way to do this is to use
graph paper, as shown in the charts in this book.
Remember that each graph square represents one
Aida block, so with 14-count Aida, 14 squares will
represent 2.5cm (1in). Start with a motif at the
centre of the band and work outwards in each
direction, adjusting the space between motifs as
necessary to finish with a complete repeat at each
end, and making sure that you leave additional
space – at least 6mm (¼in) – for turning the
ends under if, for example, the band is to be stitched
to a towel.

If you wish to fill a length exactly, you may be able
to adjust the space between repeats by inserting
extra stitches into the linking sections.

ASSEMBLY

Start by finding the centre of the band and
marking it with vertical and horizontal lines of
basting stitches. Stitch the central motif/repeat,
making sure that you leave an even space above and
below, and work out to the sides. Two strands of
cotton were used in the needle for cross stitching,
and one for backstitching.

60

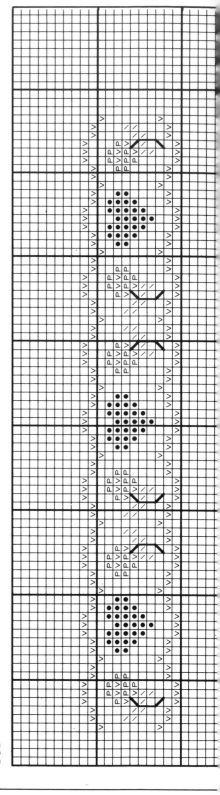

TOP

SPECIAL OCCASION BORDERS ▶	DMC	ANCHOR	MADEIRA
• White	White	02	White
● Dark salmon pink	760	09	0405
P Medium salmon pink	761	08	0404
V Pale shell pink	3713	48	0502
\ Very pale grey green	524	858	1511
S Light yellow	745	300	0111
△ Medium yellow	744	301	0112
▲ Dark golden brown	610	889	2119
R Light golden brown	612	832	2108

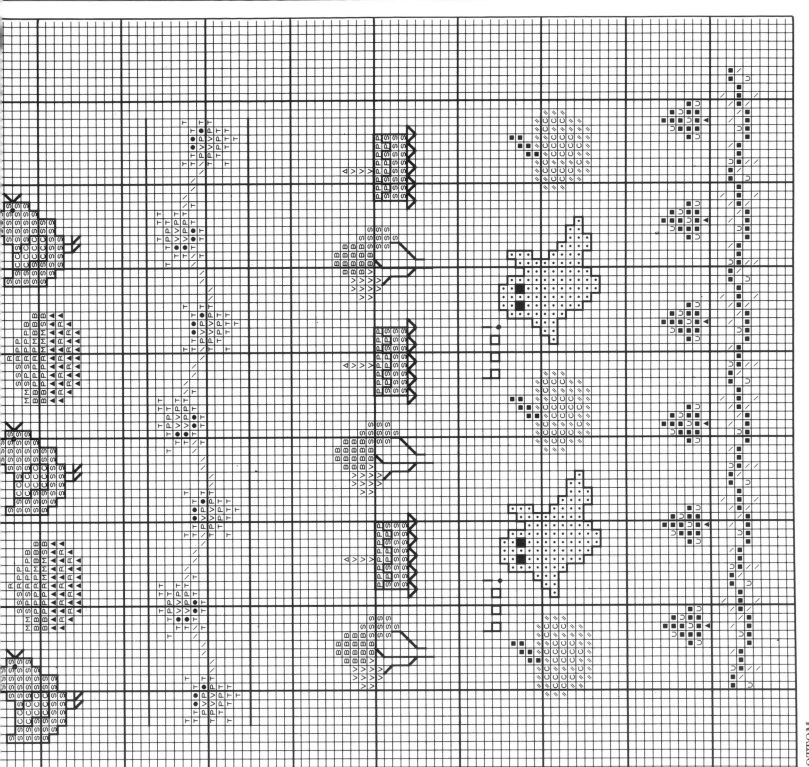

		DMC	ANCHOR	MADEIRA
T	Medium grey green	522	860	1513
B	Pale blue	3752	343	1710
M	Medium lilac	554	0711	96
■	Clear green	3363	262	1602
⁄	Medium soft orange	3776	1048	0310
C	Light orange	402	1047	2307
U	Light red	3328	1024	0406
	Dark grey*	414	233	1801

Note: backstitch the stems of Border 1 in medium grey green; the chickens of Border 2 in dark golden brown; the lines at the top and bottom of Border 3 in very pale grey green; the balloon strings, cake and lace of Border 4 and the ghost outline and lettering of Border 5 in dark grey* (used for backstitching only).

Quilted Wall Hanging

In days gone by, Christmas used to go on for twelve days and nights, until January. The song 'The First Day of Christmas' highlights this traditional time, the new line of each verse telling of an amazing gift that the lady was sent on each day.

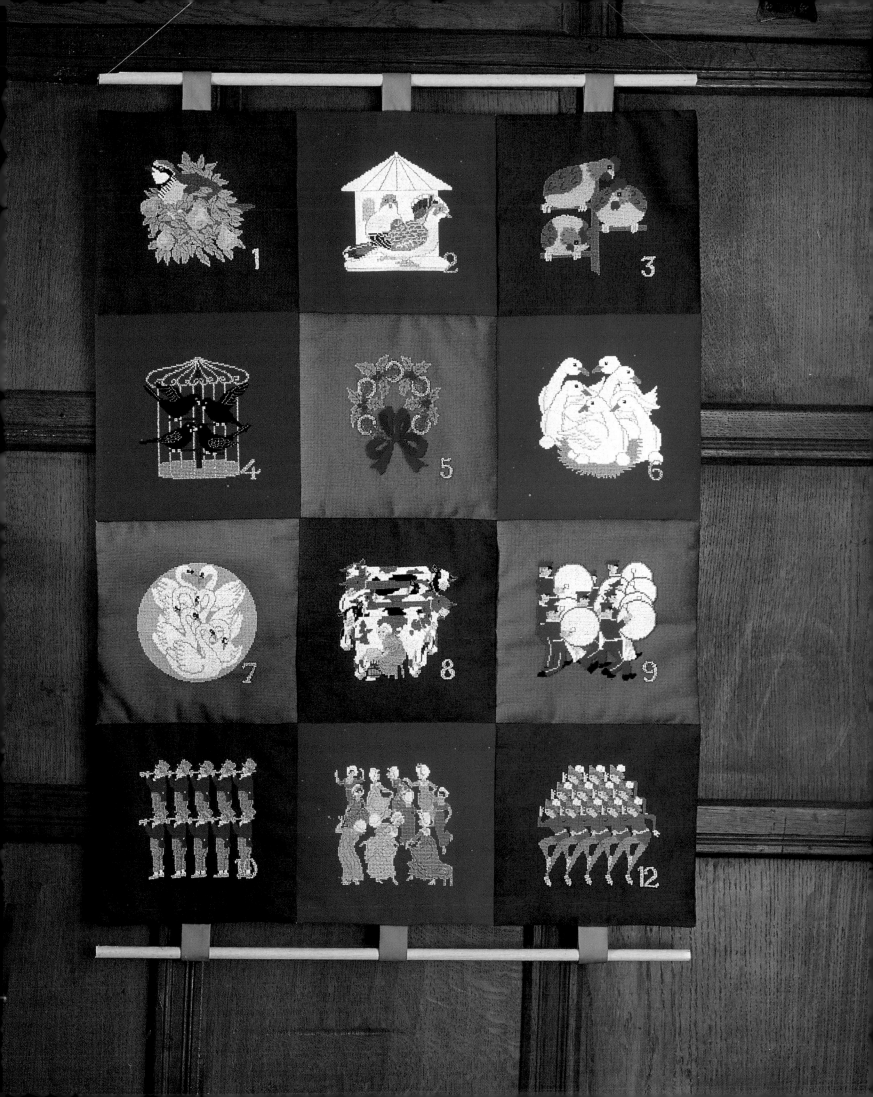

QUILTED WALL HANGING

YOU WILL NEED

For the wall hanging, measuring 61cm × 81.5cm
(24in × 32in):

*23cm (9in) squares of 18-count Aida fabric – five
of navy, four of Christmas red,
and three of holly green
71cm × 84cm (28in × 33in) of green cotton
fabric, for the backing and hanging loops
63.5cm × 84cm (25in × 33in) of thin batting
Stranded embroidery cotton in the colours given
in the appropriate panel
Gold and silver metallic threads
No26 tapestry needle
Two 60cm (23⅝in) lengths of dowling
White quilting thread*

•

THE EMBROIDERY

One by one, prepare each Aida square, marking
the centre with horizontal and vertical lines of
basting stitches, and set it in a hoop or frame (see
page 6). Embroider one of the designs on the
square, using two strands of embroidery cotton in
the needle for cross stitch, and finishing with the
backstitching, made with one strand only in the
needle. When you have embroidered all the
squares, press each finished embroidery gently on
the wrong side, using a steam iron.

MAKING THE HANGING

Position the designs as shown in the photograph.
Join the squares in horizontal rows, taking 12mm
(½in) seam allowances and pressing all seams to
one side, then join the horizontal rows. For hanging
loops, cut six strips of green cotton, each 7.7cm ×
11.5cm (3in × 4½in). Also from green fabric, cut
a piece measuring 63.5cm × 84cm (25in × 33in)
for the backing. Fold each green strip in half
lengthwise, right sides facing, and stitch down the
long side. Turn right side out and press.

Lay the backing right side down on a flat surface.
Smooth it out; place the batting on top, and then
the embroidery, right side up. Pin the three layers
together, and baste diagonally across from corner
to corner, and straight across from edge to edge,

and then in rectangles, starting close to the centre
and spaced about 10cm (4in) apart. Using the
quilting thread, quilt by hand or machine along
the lines joining the squares, stopping 2.5cm (1in)
away from the outer edge of the quilt.

Trim the batting to measure 63.5 × 84cm
(24in × 32in). Bring the edge of the backing over
the batting. Fold the hanging strips so that the short
edges meet and position three at the top and three
at the bottom of the hanging, concealing the raw
edges between the batting/backing and the top
fabric. Stitch the loops firmly to the batting/backing
layers. Fold in the raw edge of the top fabric
all around, and slipstitch in place, making sure that
the stitches do not show on the right side.

Place the lengths of dowling through the loops,
to complete your wall hanging.

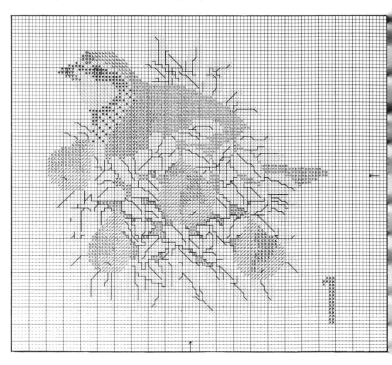

FIRST DAY OF CHRISTMAS ▲		DMC	ANCHOR	MADEIRA
II	Avocado leaf brown	830	277	2114
X	Gold thread	—	—	—
●	Black	310	403	Black
L	Light copper	922	324	0310
Z	Golden brown	977	307	2301
	Dark golden brown*	975	352	2303
C	Topaz yellow	725	306	0108
·	Light forest green	989	256	1401
	Dark green*	319	246	1313
V	Light old gold	676	891	2208
=	Dark forest green	987	245	1403
··	White	White	2	White
O	Pale grey	415	398	1803
Z	Medium copper	920	339	0312
	Very dark beaver grey*	844	401	1810

Note: backstitch golden brown in dark golden brown; light forest green
in dark green*, and medium copper in very dark beaver grey*
(starred colours used for backstitching only).*

Note: backstitch around eyes in black; other backstitching is in steel grey (used for bks only).*

Note: backstitch in medium topaz brown (used for bks only).*

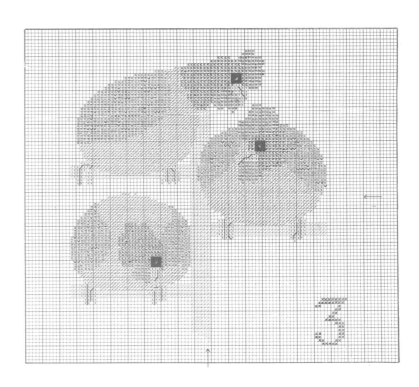

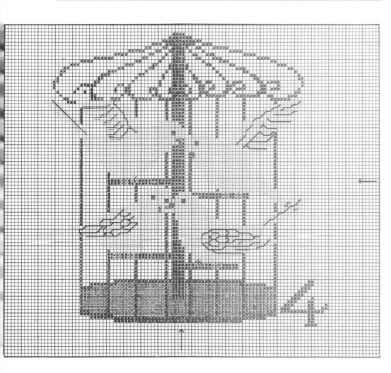

Note: backstitch with steel grey (used for bks only).*

The first day of Christmas,
my true love sent to me
A partridge in a pear tree

The second day of
Christmas, my true love
sent to me
Two turtle doves and a
partridge in a pear tree

The third day of Christmas,
my true love sent to me
Three French hens, two
turtle doves and a partridge
in a pear tree

The fourth day of
Christmas, my true love
sent to me
Four colly birds, three
French hens, etc.

The fifth day of Christmas,
my true love sent to me
Five gold rings, four colly
birds, etc.

The sixth day of Christmas,
my true love sent to me
Six geese a-laying, five
gold rings, etc

FIFTH DAY OF CHRISTMAS ▶		DMC	ANCHOR	MADEIRA
☒	Gold thread	—	—	—
Ⅲ	Medium garnet red	815	43	0513
	Dark garnet red*	814	44	0514
⃝	Bright Christmas red	666	46	0210
⃠	Christmas green	699	923	1303
⊡	Kelly green	702	226	1306
	Very dark evergreen*	890	218	1314
	Green metallic Kreinik Balger Cord* 008C			

Note: backstitch leaf veins in very dark evergreen*; around medium garnet red with dark garnet red*, and around all leaves with two strands of Kreinik green metallic* (starred colours used for bks only).

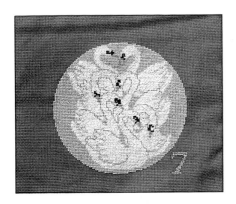

The seventh day of Christmas, my true love sent to me Seven swans a-swimming, six geese a-laying, etc

The eighth day of Christmas, my true love sent to me Eight maids a-milking, seven swans a-swimming, etc

The ninth day of Christmas, my true love sent to me Nine drummers drumming, eight maids a-milking, etc

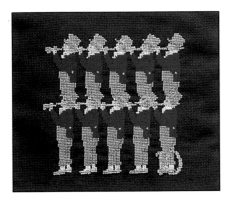

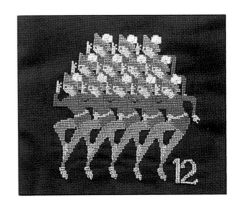

The tenth day of Christmas, my true love sent to me Ten pipers piping, nine drummers drumming, etc

The eleventh day of Christmas, my true love sent to me Eleven ladies dancing, ten pipers piping, etc

The twelfth day of Christmas, my true love sent to me Twelve lords a-leaping, eleven ladies dancing, ten pipers piping, nine drummers drumming, eight maids a-milking, seven swans a-swimming, six geese a-laying, five gold rings, four colly birds, three French hens, two turtle doves, and a partridge in a pear tree.

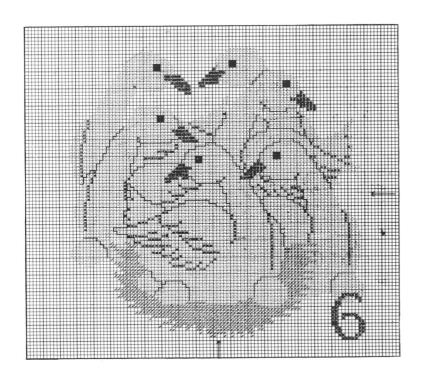

SIXTH DAY OF CHRISTMAS ◄		DMC	ANCHOR	MADEIRA
■	Black	310	403	Black
☒	Gold thread	—	—	—
⊡	White	White	2	White
	Medium steel grey*	317	400	1714
⊙	Pumpkin orange	971	316	0203
Ⅲ	Pale grey	415	398	1803
⧄	Christmas gold	783	307	2211

Note: backstitch around white with steel grey* (used for bks only).

SEVENTH DAY OF CHRISTMAS ▶

		DMC	ANCHOR	MADEIRA
[X]	Gold thread	—	—	—
[/]	Aqua	959	186	1113
[V]	Medium tangerine orange	741	304	0201
■	Black	310	403	Black
[•]	White	White	2	White
	Medium steel grey*	317	400	1714
[II]	Pale grey	415	398	1803

Note: backstitch around white steel grey (used for bks only).*

EIGHTH DAY OF CHRISTMAS ▶

		DMC	ANCHOR	MADEIRA
[X]	Gold thread	—	—	—
[/]	Medium golden brown	976	309	2302
	Very dark copper*	918	341	0314
[•]	White	White	2	White
	Light steel grey*	318	399	1802
[.•]	Light peach	754	6	0305
	Medium peach*	352	9	0303
[●]	Black	310	403	Black
[V]	Dark golden brown	975	352	2303
[\]	Delft blue	809	130	0909
	Dark Delft blue*	798	146	0911
[=]	Christmas gold	783	307	2211
[H]	Light topaz yellow	726	295	0109
[II]	Pale grey	415	398	1803
[O] [L]	Medium brown	433	371	2008
[C]	Medium pink	899	27	0505
	Very dark rose red*	326	59	0508
[I]	Golden wheat	3046	887	2206
	Dark golden wheat*	3045	888	2103
[Y]	Tan brown	436	363	2011
[◢]	Very dark coffee brown	898	360	2006
[Z]	Steel grey	414	400	1801

Note: backstitch around medium golden brown with very dark copper; around white and black with light steel grey*; around light peach with medium peach*; around Delft blue with very dark Delft blue*; around medium pink with very dark rose red*; around golden wheat with dark golden wheat*, and around tan brown with medium brown (starred colours used for bks only).*

NINTH DAY OF CHRISTMAS ▶

		DMC	ANCHOR	MADEIRA
[X]	Gold thread	—	—	—
[O]	Medium topaz brown	782	307	2212
	Dark golden brown*	975	352	2303
[●]	Black	310	403	Black
	Steel grey*	414	400	1801
[/]	Off white	746	368	0101
	Golden wheat*	3046	887	2206
[.•]	Bright orange red	606	335	0209
	Garnet red*	816	20	0512
[=]	Topaz yellow	725	306	0108
[V]	White	White	2	White
[•]	Light peach	754	6	0305
	Medium peach*	352	9	0303
■	Medium brown	433	371	2008
[II]	Pale grey	415	398	1803
[Z]	Tan brown	436	363	2011
[I]	Medium mahogany brown	301	349	2306

Note: outline medium topaz brown with dark golden brown; black with steel grey*; off white with golden wheat*; bright orange with garnet red*, and light peach with medium peach* (starred colours are used for bks only), and make the eyes with french knots in medium brown.*

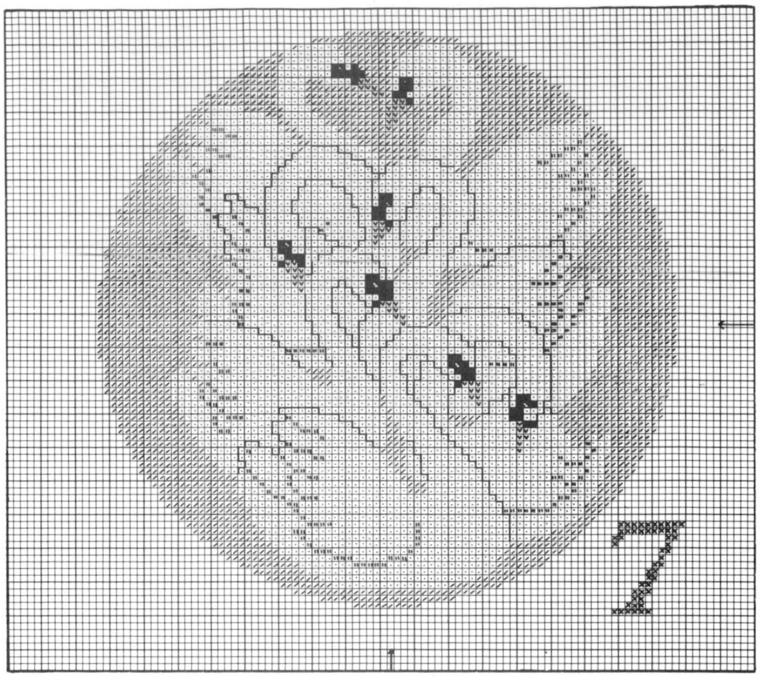

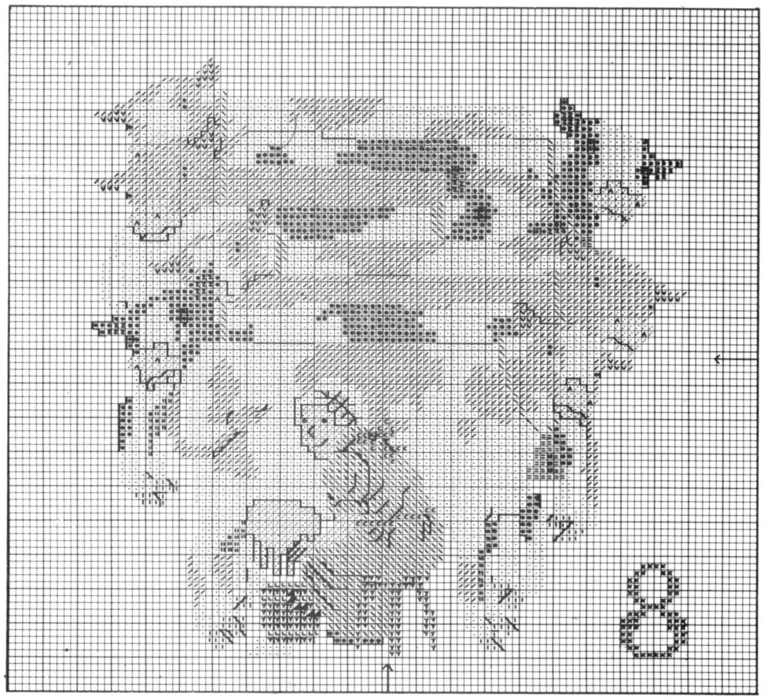

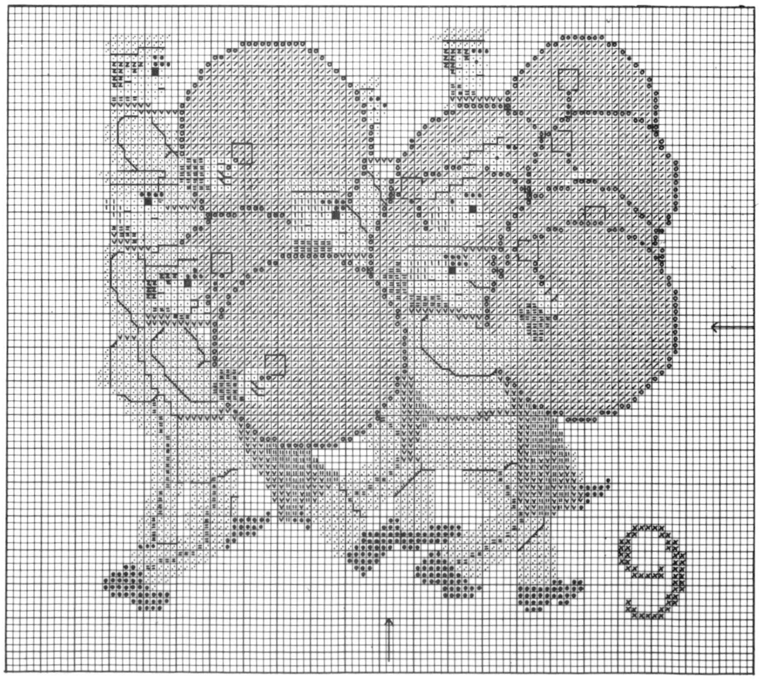

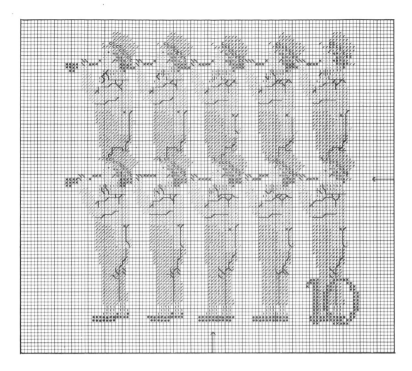

		DMC	ANCHOR	MADEIRA
⊠	Gold thread	—	—	—
⊡	Light peach	754	6	0305
	Medium peach*	352	9	0303
◉	Medium beige grey	644	830	1907
	Very dark beige grey*	640	903	1905
⊞	White	White	2	White
	Light steel grey*	318	399	1802
⊿	Light blue	813	160	1013
	Dark blue*	825	162	1011
⊡	Bright Christmas red	666	46	0210
	Dark garnet red*	814	44	0514
C	Topaz yellow	725	306	0108
Ⅲ	Tan brown	436	363	2011
⊞	Medium brown	433	371	2008

Note: outline light peach with medium peach*; medium beige grey with very dark beige grey*; white with light steel grey*; light blue with dark blue*, and bright Christmas red with dark garnet red*, and make french knots with medium brown.

		DMC	ANCHOR	MADEIRA
⊠	Gold thread	—	—	—
⊡	Light peach	754	6	0305
	Medium peach*	352	9	0303
C	Melon orange	3340	329	0214
	Medium salmon red*	3328	11	0408
⊡	Light violet	554	96	0711
	Dark violet*	552	100	0713
⊟	Light old gold	676	891	2208
	Dark old gold*	680	901	2210
☑	Silver thread	—	—	—
⊿	Aqua	959	186	1113
	Medium aqua*	943	188	1203
⊡	White	White	2	White
	Light steel grey*	318	399	1802
Z	Hazelnut brown	869	944	2105

Note: outline light peach with medium peach*; melon orange with medium salmon red*; light violet with dark violet*; light old gold with dark old gold*; aqua with medium aqua*, and white with light steel grey*, and the eyes with french knots in hazelnut brown (starred colours are used for bks only).

		DMC	ANCHOR	MADEIRA
⊠	Gold thread	—	—	—
⊡	Light peach	754	6	0305
	Medium peach*	352	9	0303
Z	Light brown	434	309	2009
⊙	Medium topaz brown	782	307	2212
⊡	White	White	2	White
	Light steel grey*	318	399	1802
⊿	Bright orange	608	333	0206
	Medium Christmas red*	304	47	0509
⊡	Kelly green	702	226	1306
	Christmas green*	699	923	1303

Note: outline light peach with medium peach*; white with light steel grey*; bright orange with medium Christmas red*, and Kelly green with Christmas green* (starred colours are used for bks only).

BABIES AND CHILDREN

Hand embroidery, on clothing, birthday cards, scatter cushions, or a toy bag, show a child how much you care and will often be treasured in a world of mass-produced goods long after that child has become an adult. The baby hand toys could even be stitched by an older child as a gift for a new brother or sister.

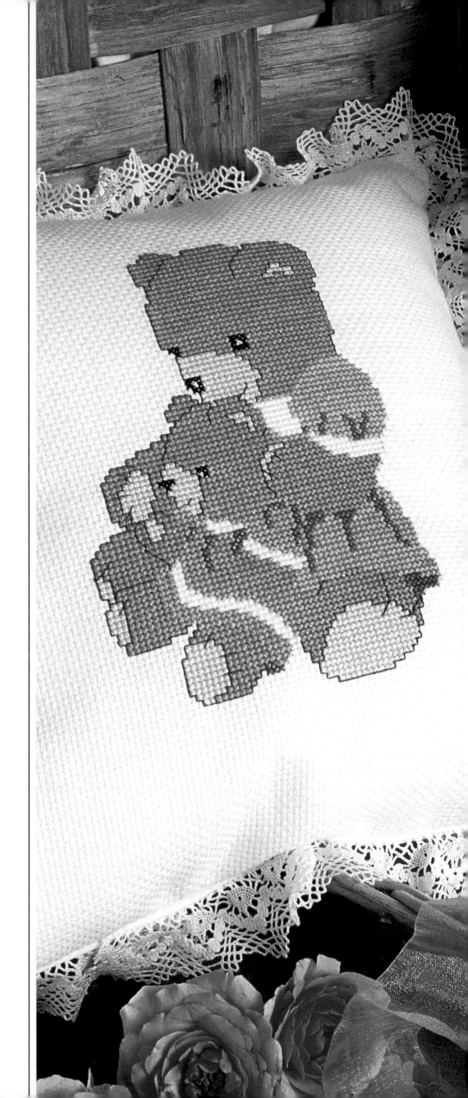

LACE-EDGED CUSHIONS

YOU WILL NEED

For each cushion, measuring 25cm (10in)
square, excluding lace edging:

*35cm (14in) square of white, 14-count Aida fabric
27.5cm (11in) square of contrast fabric,
to back your cushion
2.4m (2⅔yds) of white lace edging,
4cm (1½in) deep
Stranded embroidery cotton in the colours given
in the appropriate panel
Matching sewing thread
No24 tapestry needle
27.5cm (11in) square cushion pad*

THE EMBROIDERY

Prepare the fabric, marking the centre lines of the
design with basting stitches, and mount it in a hoop
or frame, following the instructions on page 6.
Referring to the appropriate chart, complete the
cross stitching, starting at the centre and using two
strands in the needle throughout. Embroider the
main areas first, and then finish with the backstitching, this time using a single strand in the
needle. Steam press on the wrong side.

MAKING UP THE COVER

Trim the embroidery to measure 27.5cm (11in)
square. Using a tiny french seam, join the short
edges of the lace together. Run a gathering thread
close to the straight edge; pull up the gathers to fit
and, with the right side of the embroidery facing and
the lace lying on the fabric, baste the edging to the

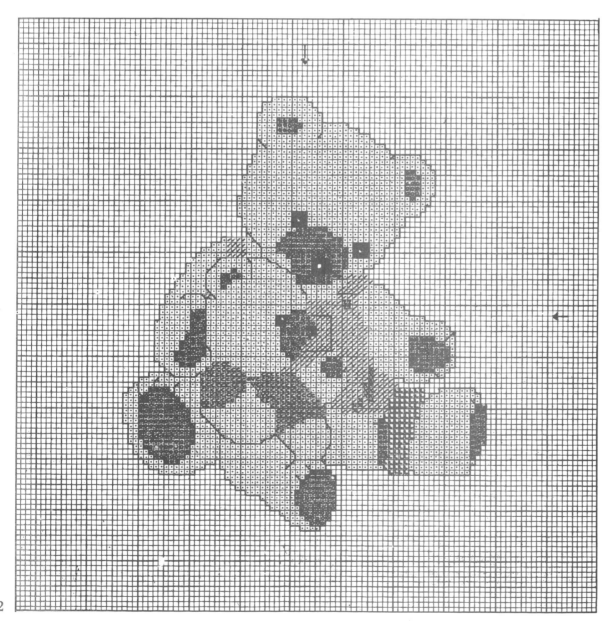

outer edge, placing it just inside the 12mm (½in) seam allowance. Adjust the gathers evenly, allowing a little extra fullness at the corners. Machine stitch the frill in place.

With right sides together, place the backing fabric on top; baste and machine stitch around, leaving a 20cm (8in) opening in the middle of one side. Remove basting stitches; trim across the corners, and turn the cover through. Insert the cushion pad and slipstitch the opening to secure it.

FATHER AND SON ◄	DMC	ANCHOR	MADEIRA
☐ White	White	2	White
c Christmas red	321	47	0510
v Garnet red	815	43	0513
L Baby blue	3325	159	1002
x Medium navy	311	148	1006
⁄ Dark baby blue	322	978	1004
o Pale golden wheat	3047	886	2205
z Medium topaz	782	307	2212
• Tan	436	363	2011
Dark coffee*	801	357	2007*
■ Black	310	403	Black

Note: dark coffee* used to backstitch around bodies, dark baby blue for trouser leg, medium navy for other clothing.

MOTHER AND DAUGHTER ▼	DMC	ANCHOR	MADEIRA
☐ White	White	2	White
⁄ Pink	3326	26	0504
• Dark pink	335	42	0506
c Medium lavender	210	104	0802
‖ Dark lavender	208	110	0804
o Pale golden wheat	3047	886	2205
• Tan	436	363	2011
Dark coffee*	801	357	2007*
Light grey*	415	398	1803
■ Black	310	403	Black

Note: dark coffee* used to backstitch around bodies, light grey* for sleeve.

Baby Hand-toys

Nursery animals, just big enough for small hands to hold, are embroidered on one side only in colourful cross stitch patterns.

These easy-to-sew shapes are gently padded to give roundness and softness, and when a toy is not being held by baby, it can be hung at the side of the crib by its ribbon loop.

BABY HAND-TOYS

YOU WILL NEED

For three hand toys, each measuring
approximately 13cm × 9cm (5in × 3½in):

*Six 18cm × 13cm (7¼in × 5in) rectangles of
white, 22-count Hardanger; two pieces for each toy
Stranded embroidery cotton in the colours
given in the panels
Sufficient loose synthetic filling for each toy
90cm (1yd) of white satin ribbon, 6mm (¼in) wide
No26 tapestry needle
Matching sewing thread
Three 15cm × 10cm (6in × 4in) pieces of
cardboard (use a breakfast cereal box, or
similar packaging)
Tracing paper*

•

THE EMBROIDERY

All three toys are embroidered and made up in the
same way. For each toy, prepare one of the two pieces
of evenweave fabric and stretch it in a frame, see
page 7. Following the appropriate chart, complete
the cross stitching, using two strands of thread in the
needle throughout, and working one cross stitch over
two threads of ground fabric. Steam press on the
wrong side, if needed.

MAKING UP THE TOYS

Trace the outline of the appropriate toy; transfer it to
the cardboard, marking the position of the arrows.
Cut out the template; centre it on the wrong side of
the embroidery, matching the edges of the cross
stitching and aligning the arrows. Draw round the
shape with a pencil.

Working freehand, draw a second (cutting) line
6mm (¼in) beyond the first pencil (stitching) line. Do
not cut out the toy shape at this stage; the fabric
tends to fray during sewing, and it is therefore best to
complete the stitching first.

Cut the ribbon into three equal lengths; set two
aside for the remaining toys, and fold one length in
half. Place the back and embroidered front fabrics
right sides together. With the cut ends of the ribbon
protruding just beyond the raw edges of the fabric,
lay the folded ribbon between the two sections, as
marked on the chart.

With the ribbon inside, pin and baste the sections
together, stitching between the two marked lines.
Using matching sewing thread, either machine stitch
or backstitch around the edge, sewing on the seamline and leaving a small opening for the filling, as
indicated on the chart.

Cut out, following the outer pencil line. Snip into
any curves, taking care not to cut the seam. Remove
the basting stitches and turn the toy through to the
right side. Steam press, and then finger press the
seam flat.

Gently fill the toy, using a knitting needle to
push small amounts of the filling into awkward
shapes, such as the cat's ears. Turn in the edges of
the opening and slipstitch to close.

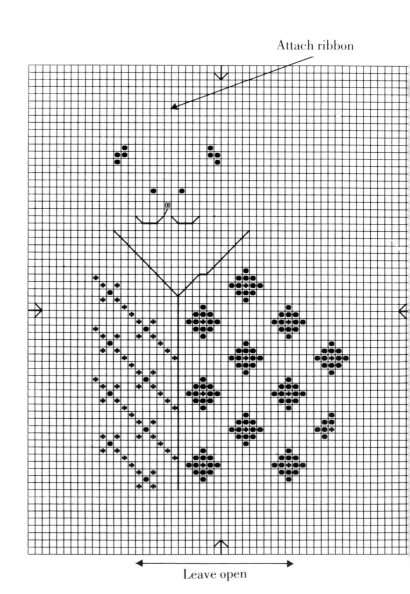

Attach ribbon

Leave open

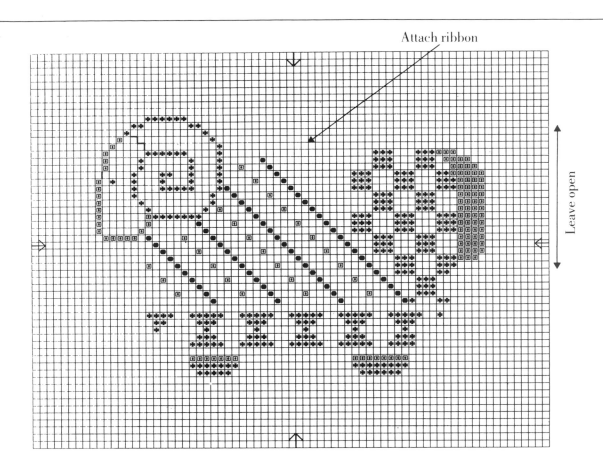

Attach ribbon

Leave open

RAM ▲	ANCHOR	DMC	MADEIRA
⊡ Very pale green	213	504	1309
● Pink	26	3733	0609
✠ Sea green	167	597	1109

Note: backstitch the horns in sea green.

TEDDY ▶	ANCHOR	DMC	MADEIRA
⊡ Medium yellow	301	744	0112
● Ochre	844	833	2203
✠ Olive green	267	581	1408

Note: backstitch shirt and trousers in olive green.

CAT ◀	ANCHOR	DMC	MADEIRA
✠ Red	11	3705	0411
● Light blue	977	334	0909
⊡ Deep blue	146	798	0911

Note: backstitch mouth and around body in deep blue.

Attach ribbon

Leave open

77

Baby's Coverlet

Could any tiny child, or mother, resist the enchantment of these lovely sleepy teddies? This wonderfully soft and practical Afghan fabric, featuring 13cm (5in) squares, is ideal for a baby's coverlet, and easily washable.

BABY'S COVERLET

YOU WILL NEED

For a coverlet, measuring 86cm × 104cm
(34in × 41in):

92cm × 110cm (37in × 44in) of
Anne Afghan fabric
Stranded embroidery cotton in the colours given in
the panel; two skeins of tan are required
Matching cream sewing thread
No26 tapestry needle

•

THE EMBROIDERY

Following the diagram, cut the fabric to size. If you
are securing the fringe by machine, stitch a zigzag
border all around, as indicated. Mark the centre
lines of each design with basting stitches, and
mount the fabric in a hoop, following the instructions on page 7. Referring to the appropriate chart,
complete each design, starting at the centre of each

and using two strands in the needle for cross stitching and one for backstitched lines.

COMPLETING THE COVERLET

Trim the fabric to the final size. To make the fringe,
either remove fabric threads one at a time until you
reach the zigzag stitch line, or hemstitch, as shown.
Brush out the fringe with a stiff brush.

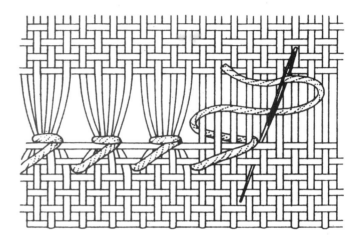

HEMSTITCH

Remove a single thread from the fabric at the hem-
line (the start of the fringe). Bring the needle out on
the right side, two threads below the drawn-thread
line. Working from left to right, pick up from two to
four threads, as shown in the diagram. Bring the
needle out again and insert it behind the fabric, to
emerge two threads down, ready to make the next
stitch. Before reinserting the needle, pull the thread
tight, so that the bound threads form a neat group. To
complete the fringe, remove the weft threads below
the hemstitching.

BABY'S COVERLET ▶	DMC	ANCHOR	MADEIRA
L White	White	2	White
∴ Medium lavender	210	104	0802
● Dark carnation	891	29	0411
I Delft blue	809	130	0909
x Light emerald	912	209	1212
╱ Very light yellow	3078	292	0102
o Light topaz	727	293	0110
c Very light brown	435	365	2010
v Light brown	434	309	2009
· Tan	436	363	2011
∧ Light grey	415	398	1803
Steel grey*	317	400	1714
Dark steel grey*	413	401	1713
Black*	310	403	Black

Note: black* used for backstitched clock hands, clock numbers steel
grey*, all outlines dark steel grey*.

Final cutting line   Final cutting line

Final cutting line

Design
1

Zigzag border

Design   Design
2   2

Design
1

Design   Design
3   3

Final cutting line

104cm
(41in)

← 86cm (34in) →

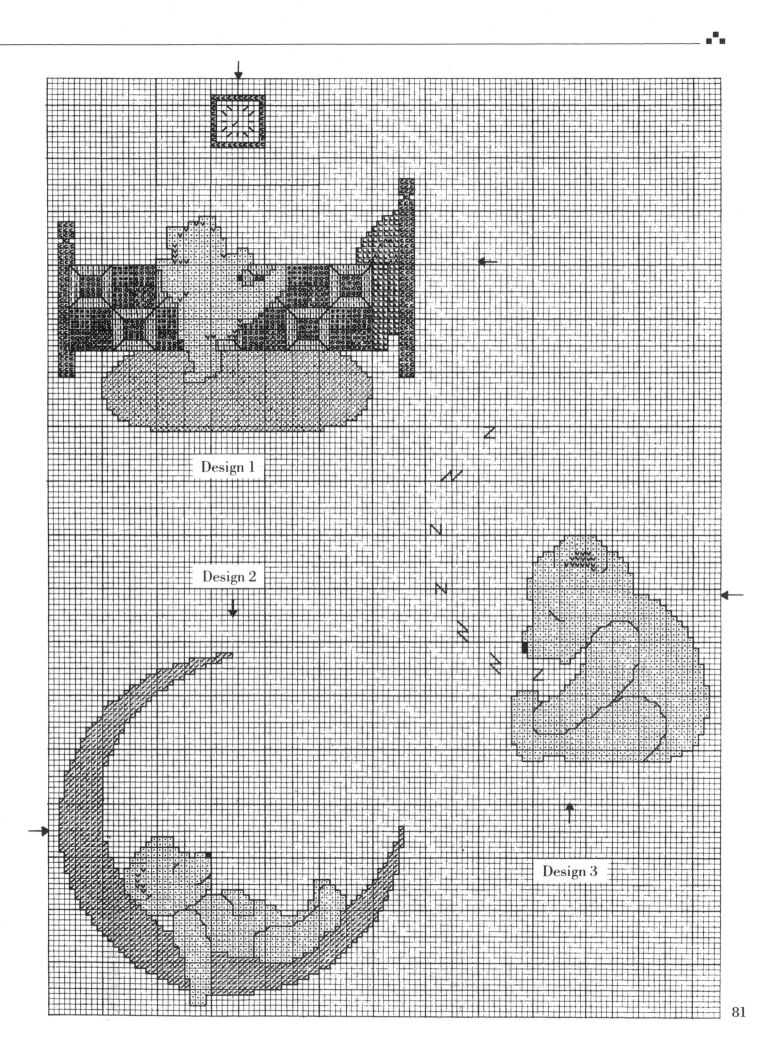

Design 1

Design 2

Design 3

Toy Bag

Suitable for a child of any age group, this toy bag will make an extremely practical gift, and a bright and attractive feature in the playroom or nursery. The bag has a draw-string top and is both large enough and strong enough to hold many small toys.

TOY BAG

YOU WILL NEED

For a toy bag, measuring 60cm × 44cm
(24in × 17½in):

*65cm (26in) of cream pearl Aida fabric, 110cm
(43in) wide, with 11 threads to 2.5cm (1in)
65cm (26in) of firm, unbleached cotton (calico),
110cm (43in) wide, for the lining
250cm (2½yds) of white cord, 6mm (¼in)
in diameter
Stranded embroidery cotton in the colours
given in the panel
Matching sewing thread
No24 tapestry needle*

•

THE EMBROIDERY

Take a piece of fabric measuring 65cm × 50cm
(26in × 20in). Prepare the fabric, marking the
centre lines of the design with basting stitches;
ensure that there is a clearance around the design
area of 15.5cm (6½in) at the sides and bottom, and
26cm (10¼in) at the top, and mount it in a hoop
or frame, following the instructions on page 6.
Referring to the chart, complete the cross stitching,
using three strands in the needle throughout.
Embroider the main areas first, and then finish with
the backstitching, this time using two strands of
thread in the needle. If necessary, steam press on
the wrong side.

MAKING THE BAG

Trim the edges of the embroidered fabric until the
piece measures 47cm × 63.5cm (18½in × 25in),
with a clearance around the design of 14cm (5½in)
at the sides and bottom and 25.5cm (10in) from the
top. Cut a second piece of Aida fabric to match.

With right sides together and taking a 12mm
(½in) seam allowance, stitch the side seams,
stitching down from the top for 5cm (2in), leaving a
gap of 3.5cm (1¼in), and then continuing to the
bottom (A).

Join the bottom seam. Press the seams flat and
topstitch around each gap, 6mm (¼in) from the
pressed edge, as shown (B).

Cut two lining pieces, each measuring 47cm ×
62.5cm (18½in × 24½in). Place the two pieces of
lining fabric with right sides together and stitch the

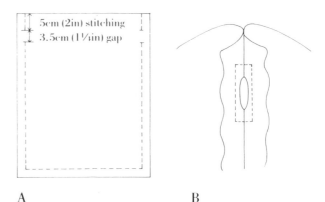

A   B

side seams (all the way), and then the bottom seam,
leaving an opening of 15cm (6in) for turning (C).

Place the outer bag into the lining, with right sides
together, and stitch around the top edge. Press
seams flat, then turn the bag right side out through
the opening. Slipstitch the opening to close it. Press
around the top of the bag, then topstitch two lines,
6mm (¼in) above and below the side openings (D).
Thread the cord twice through the resulting case-
ment and tie the ends together.

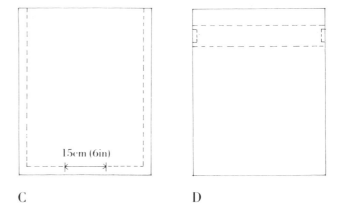

C   D

TOY BAG ▶		DMC	ANCHOR	MADEIRA
□	White	White	2	White
V	Garnet	816	20	0512
↳	Dark Christmas red	498	47	0511
–	Lemon yellow	307	289	0104
T	Christmas gold	783	307	2211
＼	Tangerine	740	316	0202
╱	Bright orange	606	335	0209
∧	Baby blue	3325	159	1002
=	Medium baby blue	334	161	1003
C	Dark baby blue	322	978	1004
X	Aquamarine	992	187	1202
•	Royal blue	797	132	0912
H	Medium navy	311	148	1006
‖	Dark emerald	910	228	1310
O	Very light tan	738	942	2013
•	Tan	436	363	2011
•	Medium topaz	782	307	2212
Z	Light brown	434	309	2009
L	Dark coffee	801	357	2007
	Very dark beaver*	844	401	1810
■	Black	310	403	Black

Note: very dark beaver* used for all backstitch outlines.

Animal Alphabet

These striking designs would bring a smile to the face of any child. Take your child's initial and either embroider this on its own or combine it with backstitching in a lower case alphabet to make the fullname

ANIMAL ALPHABET

YOU WILL NEED

For the card, measuring 20cm × 15cm
(8in × 6in), with an oval aperture measuring
15cm × 10cm (6in × 4in):

*25cm × 20cm (10in × 8in) of 14-count,
white Aida fabric
Stranded embroidery cotton in the colours given
in the panel
No24 tapestry needle
Card, for suppliers see page 144*

For the framed initial, here in a frame measuring
15cm × 11.5cm (6in × 4½in), with an aperture
measuring 13cm × 10cm (5¼in × 4in):

*20cm × 15cm (8in × 6in) of 14-count, white
Aida fabric
Stranded embroidery cotton in the colours given
in the panel
No24 tapestry needle
Frame of your choice*

*NOTE: the letters vary in size, and can be
worked on virtually any evenweave fabric.
To calculate the dimensions of your chosen
initial(s), divide the maximum number of stitches
each way by the count of the fabric (the number
of blocks/stitches per 2.5cm/1in)*

For the bib, measuring 18.5cm × 15cm
(7⅜in × 6in):

*Stranded embroidery cotton in the colours given
in the panel
No24 tapestry needle
Evenweave bib, for suppliers see page 144*

To embroider initials on purchased
(non-evenweave) clothes:

*Stranded embroidery cotton in the colours given
in the panel
No24 tapestry needle
Zweigart's waste 14-count canvas,
a piece 5cm (2in) larger each way than the
dimensions of the finished embroidered initial
Fine tweezers
Water spray
Basting cotton and needle
Chosen item of clothing*

THE CARD

Prepare the fabric, marking the centre with horizontal and vertical lines of basting stitches. Mount it in a hoop as explained on page 6. Start the stitching at the centre, using two strands of cotton in the needle, if using 14-count Aida (see Stitching details). Take each stitch over one block of fabric in each direction, making sure that all the top crosses run in the same direction and that each row is worked into the same holes as the top or bottom of the row before, so that you do not leave a space between rows.

MAKING UP

Gently steam press the embroidery on the wrong side and trim it to measure 12mm (½in) larger each way than the aperture. Centre your embroidery behind the opening and secure it in place with double-sided tape. Press the card firmly together.

THE FRAMED INITIAL

The embroidery is worked in the same way as for the card. Gently steam press the finished embroidery on the wrong side; mount it (see page 9), and set it in a frame of your choice.

THE BIB

Mark the centre of the bib with horizontal and vertical lines of basting stitches, and embroider your chosen initial (see individual stitching details), using two strands of embroidery cotton in the needle and taking each stitch over one block of the fabric.

When you have finished, remove the basting stitches and gently steam press the bib on the wrong side.

USING WASTE CANVAS

Position the blue threads of the canvas horizontally or vertically with the weave of the garment. Pin and then baste the canvas in place and remove the pins. Each pair of canvas threads is treated as one thread, so the cross stitch is worked over one pair of threads in each direction. Start stitching in the centre, which you can mark on the canvas with a vertical and horizontal line of basting stitches. Begin the embroidery by fastening the cotton with your first stitches, and finish by threading the cotton through a few stitches at the back of the work. Make sure that you start and finish firmly, so that the stitches do not pull out during washing.

When the cross stitching is complete, trim the

canvas to within 12mm (½in) of the embroidery. Dampen the embroidery on the right side with warm water and leave for a few minutes until the threads soften. Using tweezers, pull the canvas threads out one at a time so that you do not damage your embroidery.

Press the embroidery by placing it right side down on a towel and pressing with a hot iron and damp cloth.

ALPHABET STITCHING DETAILS

All letters are worked using three strands of stranded cotton for 11-count fabric, two for 14-count fabric and one for 18- or 22-count fabric.

All outlining is in backstitch, using one strand of dark grey unless stated otherwise. Additional stitching details are as follows:

The letter B
Embroider the bee's wings in backstitch with one strand of dark grey.

The letter C
Embroider the whiskers in backstitch with two strands of black cotton.

The letters E and J
Embroider the water in backstitch with two strands of dark blue.

The letter I
Embroider the feelers in backstitch, using two strands of black cotton.

The letter L
Embroider the feelers in backstitch, using two strands of black cotton.

The letter R
Embroider the whiskers in backstitch with one strand of dark grey cotton.

The letter S
Embroider the whiskers in straight stitch with one strand of black cotton.

The letter U
Embroider the tufts of hair in backstitch with two strands of yellow cotton.

The letter V
Embroider the vipers' tongue in backstitch, using two strands of black cotton.

The letter W
Embroider the water in backstitch with two strands of pale blue.

ANIMAL ALPHABET		DMC	ANCHOR	MADEIRA
C	Light gold	676	887	2208
V	Dark gold	729	890	2209
/	Light brown	437	362	2011
=	Medium brown	435	(363)	2009
Z	Dark brown	434	365	2008
X	Moss green	471	265	(1501)
S	Light jade green	563	208	1207
W	Dark jade green	562	210	(1206)
r	Red	349	(46)	0212
·	Yellow	743	301	0109
e	Light blue	800	128	1014
n	Dark blue	799	130	1012
+	Light grey	318	235	1802
>	Medium grey	414	399	1801
–	Pink	604	60	(0614)
a	Mauve	340	118	0902
*	Black	Black	403	Black
0	White	White	1	White
	Dark grey*	3799	(236)	(1713)

Note: numbers in brackets indicate the nearest colour match; for backstitched outline use dark grey (used for bks only).*

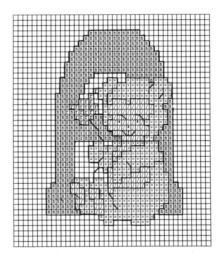

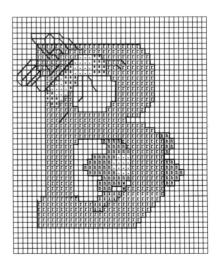

Turn to page 92 for charts for the remaining letters.

89

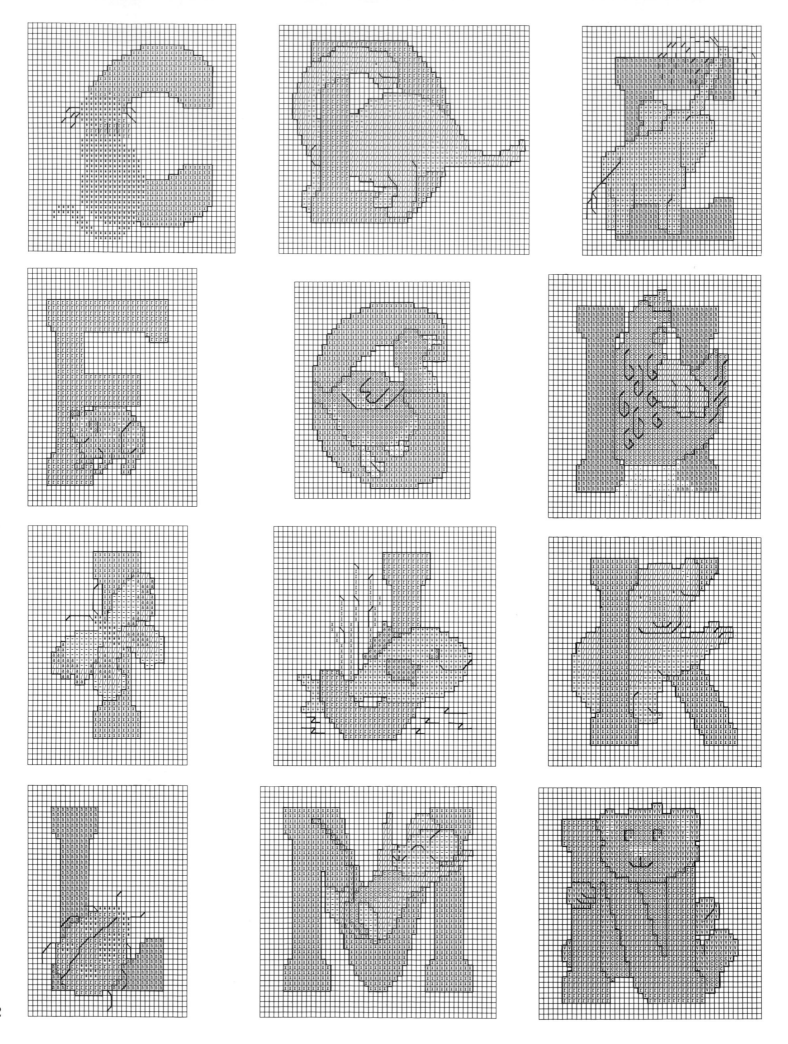

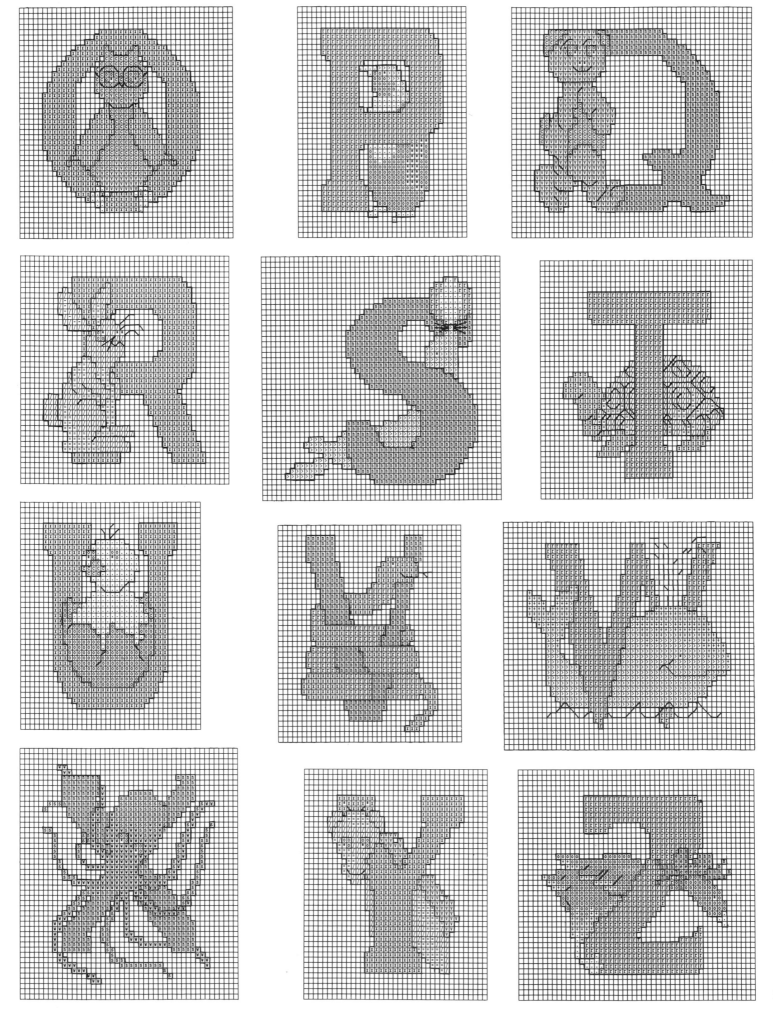

Decorative Motifs

Even the plainest of children's clothes can be turned into something rather special with the addition of these small, attractive motifs.

DECORATIVE MOTIFS

YOU WILL NEED

To embroider either of these decorations on your chosen item of children's clothing:

Zweigart's waste, 14-count canvas (for suppliers, see page 144), as below – for Kite Bear, 23cm × 18cm (9in × 7¼in); for Bears and Hearts, a strip of canvas 10cm (4in) deep and the desired length of the border
Stranded embroidery cotton in the colours given in the appropriate panel
No24 tapestry needle
Fine tweezers
Water spray bottle

•

THE EMBROIDERY

To ensure that your finished embroidery lies straight on the garment, align the blue threads horizontally or vertically, either with the weave of the fabric or with the seams of the garment, whichever is appropriate. Pin the canvas centrally over the area where the design is to be stitched, and baste it in place around the edges. Remove the pins.

Treat each pair of canvas threads as a single thread, and stitch the design as you would on any other evenweave fabric. Start stitching at the top of the design and work downwards, using two strands for the cross stitch, and one for the backstitch.

You can start and finish threads as usual, by anchoring with your first few stitches, and threading the ends of the threads in on the back of the work when you finish. If the garments are going to be laundered frequently, you may want to begin and end threads with a small knot for added security.

When you have completed your cross stitch embroidery, cut away the extra canvas, leaving approximately 12mm (½in) all around the design. Dampen the right side with slightly warm water (do not soak it) and leave it for a few minutes until the sizing softens. Use tweezers to pull each of the canvas threads out one at a time. Moisten again if required. Resist the temptation to pull out more than one thread at a time, as you may damage your embroidery.

As if by magic, you are now left with the finished design on your garment. Place your embroidered garment wrong side up over a dry towel and press, being careful not to flatten the stitches.

If you choose to sew your design onto fabric which is dry-cleanable only, the canvas threads can be softened by rubbing them together (taking care not to damage the embroidery). It should then be possible to remove the threads one by one without having to use water.

BEARS AND HEARTS ▼		DMC	ANCHOR	MADEIRA
•	Deep rose	309	42	0507
∕	Christmas gold	783	307	2211
■	Black	310	403	Black

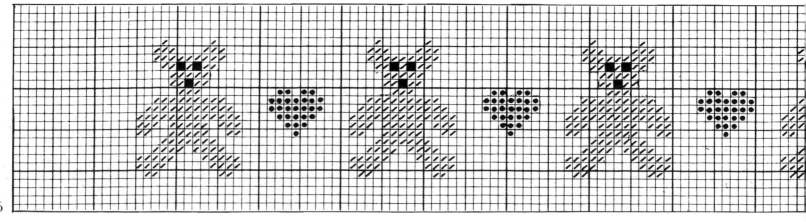

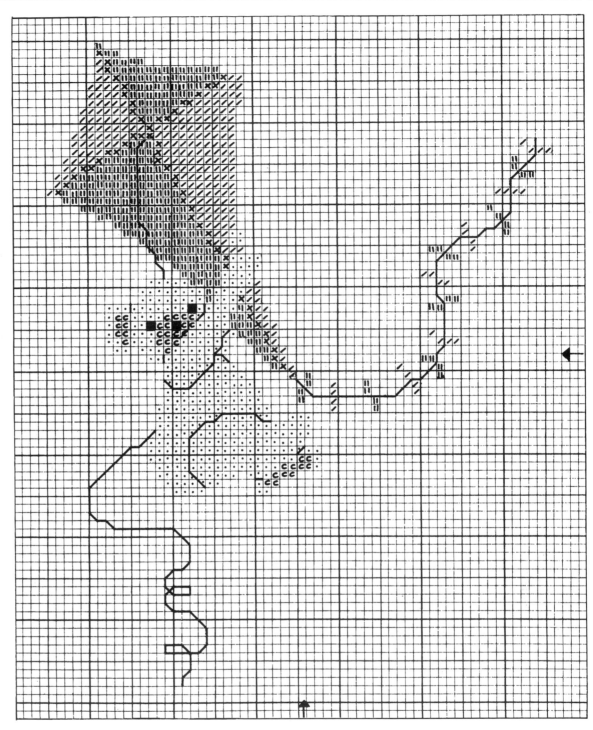

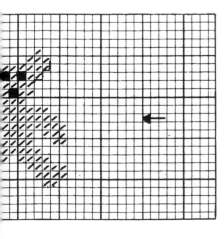

KITE BEAR ▲	DMC	ANCHOR	MADEIRA
╱ Pink	3326	26	0504
‖ Delft blue	809	130	0909
c Pale old gold	677	886	2207
x Light old gold	676	891	2208
• Medium beige	3032	888	2104
Grey brown*	3022	8581	1903
Dark grey brown*	3021	382	1904
■ Black	310	403	Black

Note: use dark grey brown* for backstitched outline of bear and dark grey brown* for kite.

Dressing-Table Set

What little girl could resist the charm of this silver-plated set of hairbrush and mirror? Two complementary designs make this a delightful gift for a teddy fan.

DRESSING-TABLE SET

No26 tapestry needle
Dressing-table set (for suppliers, see page 144)

•

YOU WILL NEED

For the dressing-table set – handmirror with back, measuring 13cm × 11.5cm (5in × 4½in), hairbrush with back, measuring 10cm × 9cm (4in × 3½in):

44cm × 22cm (17in × 8½in) of white, 22-count Hardanger fabric
Iron-on interfacing (optional) –
two pieces, one measuring
14cm × 13cm (5½in × 5¼in) and one
11cm × 10cm (4¼in × 4in)
Stranded embroidery cotton in the colours given in the appropriate panels

THE EMBROIDERY

Both designs are stitched in the same way and on the same type of fabric. You may be able to economize on fabric by using one large piece, remembering to allow sufficient space between the pictures.

Prepare the fabric, marking the centre lines of each design with basting stitches, and mount it in a hoop or frame, following the instructions on page 7. Referring to the appropriate chart and starting at the centre, complete the cross stitching, using one strand in the needle throughout. Embroider the main areas first, and then finish with the backstitching. Steam press on the wrong side.

BUTTERFLY BEAR ▶	DMC	ANCHOR	MADEIRA
□ White	White	2	White
╱ Medium violet	553	98	0712
C Dark violet	550	101	0714
• Christmas gold	783	307	2211
‖ Dark topaz	780	309	2214
● Dark coffee	801	357	2007
X Dark beaver	645	400	1811
■ Black	310	403	Black

Note: dark beaver also used for bks.

It is a good idea to leave the basting stitches in at this stage, as they will prove useful in helping to centre your design in the frame.

ASSEMBLING THE DRESSING-TABLE SET

If you prefer to use iron-on interfacing to avoid wrinkles, first iron a piece of the appropriate size to the back of each embroidery, transferring the registration marks as described for the cards on page 48. If you are not using interfacing, leave the basting stitches in at this stage.

The paper templates supplied by the manufacturers may vary in size so, in order to get an exact fit for each piece, cut out the embroidery, using the template supplied with each piece, but first mark the centre on the template both ways in pencil. In each case, place the template with the marked side on the wrong side of the embroidery; match the pencil lines to the basting stitches, and draw around with a soft pencil. This will help you to centre your embroidery.

Before cutting out, place the template inside the particular frame and check to see how much more fabric, if any, should be included beyond the pencil line. This is a critical stage in the assembly, because the return on the frames is very shallow and therefore does not allow for adjustment if the fabric has been cut too small.

When you are satisfied, cut out the fabric and remove any remaining basting stitches.

Complete the assembly of both pieces, following the manufacturer's instructions.

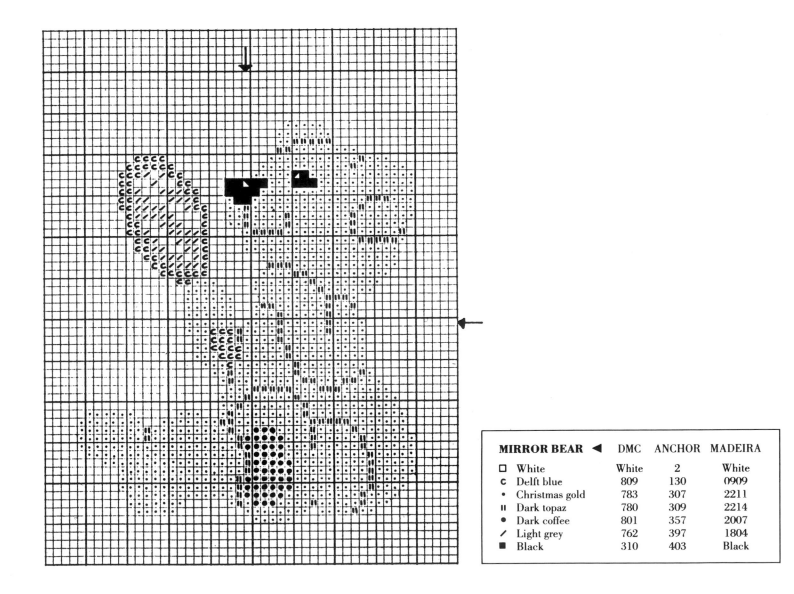

MIRROR BEAR ◄	DMC	ANCHOR	MADEIRA
□ White	White	2	White
c Delft blue	809	130	0909
• Christmas gold	783	307	2211
‖ Dark topaz	780	309	2214
● Dark coffee	801	357	2007
╱ Light grey	762	397	1804
■ Black	310	403	Black

DECORATIVE TOUCHES

*A touch of hand-embroidery here
and there around the house
creates a caring and elegant
effect, giving a home-like feeling.
The projects in this section include
the knitting bag featured here,
tea towels, trinket boxes, a pair of
beautiful cushions, paperweights,
a tray and a host of designs that
could be used for a wide range
of projects.*

KNITTING BAG

For each knitting bag, measuring
36.5cm × 32cm (14½in × 12½in):

42cm × 76cm (16½in × 30in) of cream,
14-count Aida fabric
42cm × 76cm (16½in × 30in) of thin
polyester batting
42cm × 76cm (16½in × 30in) of calico,
for the lining
Stranded embroidery cotton in the colours given in
the appropriate panels
No26 tapestry needle
Sewing thread to match the fabric
A pair of handles (for suppliers, see page 144)

•

THE EMBROIDERY

Fold the embroidery fabric in half; press and
unfold. Taking the top (bag front) section, mark the
centre lines with basting stitches (see page 6) and
set it in a frame. Complete the cross stitching,
using two strands of thread in the needle, and then
the backstitching, using one strand. Ensure that
there is approximately 9cm (3½in) clearance at each
side of the finished embroidery (front section), 2.5cm
(1in) at the bottom, and 12.5cm (5in) at
the top.

Gently steam press the embroidered fabric on the
wrong side.

MAKING THE BAG

Pin, baste and stitch the batting to the wrong side
of the embroidered fabric, stitching around all sides
and taking a 1cm (½in) seam allowance. Trim the
batting back to the stitching line. Fold the fabric
in half, with right sides facing, and pin and baste
the side seams, taking a 1cm (½in) seam allowance
Stitch the side seams, stopping 16.5cm (6½in)
short of the top edge at each side.

Fold the lining in half, with right sides facing,
and stitch the side seams, as for the main fabric.
Turn the main fabric right side out and place the
lining inside the bag. Turn in the 12mm (½in)
allowance around the remaining raw edges and top
stitch them together, making sure that no lining is
visible on the right side. Thread the top edges of
the bag through the bag handles, gathering the
fabric evenly, and catch-stitch by hand to finish.

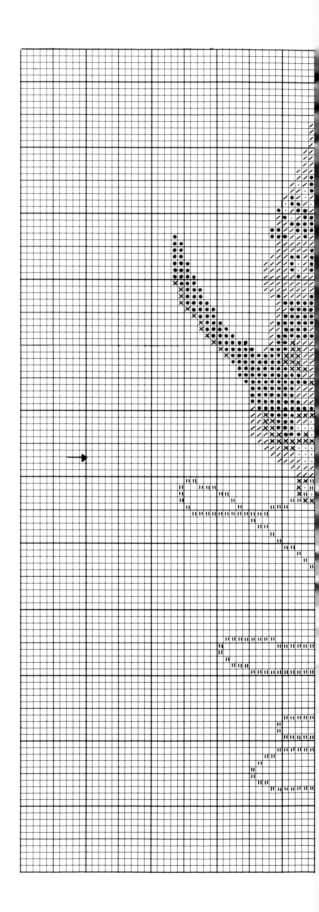

KNITTING BAG ▼		DMC	ANCHOR	MADEIRA
⊙	Dark steel grey	413	401	1713
⊠	Steel grey	414	400	1801
◢	Pale grey	415	398	1803
⊡	White	White	2	White
⊞	Medium pink	899	27	0505

Note: backstitch outline in pale grey.

Village Ducks Bath Set

Ducklings waddle behind their
mother along a towel border and
across the flap of a make-up purse.
This charming design would also
make a pretty greetings card
for any occasion.

VILLAGE DUCKS
BATH SET

YOU WILL NEED

For the towel border:

*52cm (20¾in) length of 5cm (2in) white Aida band
with yellow edging
Stranded embroidery cotton in the colours given
in the panel
No24 tapestry needle
Hand towel
Matching thread*

For the make-up purse, measuring 17cm × 13.5cm
(6¾in × 5⅜in) when closed:

*45cm × 25cm (18in × 10in) blue,
14-count Aida fabric
Stranded embroidery cotton in the colours given
in the panel
No24 tapestry needle
38cm × 17cm (15¼in x 6¾in) cotton lining fabric
85cm (4in) yellow cotton bias binding,
1.5cm (⅝in) wide
Matching thread*

●

THE EMBROIDERY

Stretch the fabric in a hoop or frame, as explained on page 7. Following the appropriate chart, work each embroidery using two strands of embroidery cotton in the needle. Work each stitch over one block of fabric in each direction. Make sure the top crosses run in the same direction.

For the make-up purse, position the design at one end of the fabric and stitch your chosen initials in the area indicated. Gently steam press the finished embroideries on the wrong side.

MAKING THE TOWEL BORDER

Fold in 12mm (½in) at each end of the Aida band. Pin the strip in place across the width of the towel (covering the area that has no pile). With matching sewing thread, hand-stitch the band in place.

MAKING THE MAKE-UP PURSE

Place the lining fabric, right side up, centrally over the back of the embroidery. Baste the two together

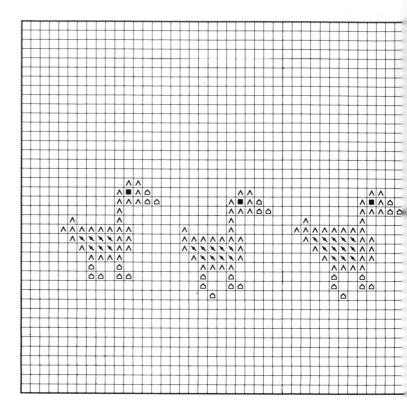

close to the edge of the lining fabric. Trim the Aida to match the size of the lining. Cut a 17cm (6¾in) length of bias binding and use it to bind the short end, furthest away from the embroidered area. Handstitch in place. Fold up this end to form a pocket. The embroidered part will form the flap of the purse; cut the corners to a neat, rounded shape. Now use the rest of the bias binding to bind the remaining raw edges.

TOWEL BORDER ▲		DMC	ANCHOR	MADEIRA
⊡	White	White	1	White
■	Black	310	403	Black
⊠	Dark grey	317	400	1714
⊟	Mid grey	415	399	1803
⊥	Pale grey	762	234	1804
∧	Pale yellow	727	289	103
◥	Yellow	444	297	105
△	Orange	742	313	2307

MAKE-UP PURSE ▶		DMC	ANCHOR	MADEIRA
⊡	White	White	1	White
■	Black	310	403	Black
⊠	Dark grey	317	400	1714
⊟	Mid grey	415	399	1803
⊥	Pale grey	762	234	1804
∧	Pale steel	3752	1038	1105
△	Tan brown	782	901	2210
◥	Pale yellow	727	289	103
+	Yellow	444	297	105
⊙	Orange	742	313	2307
⊠	Steel blue	931	779	1712

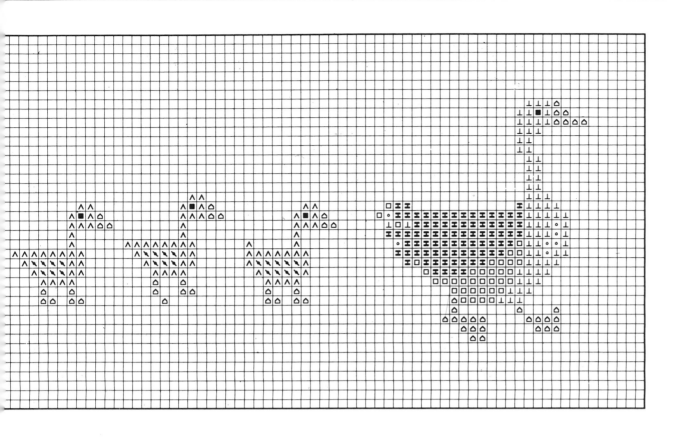

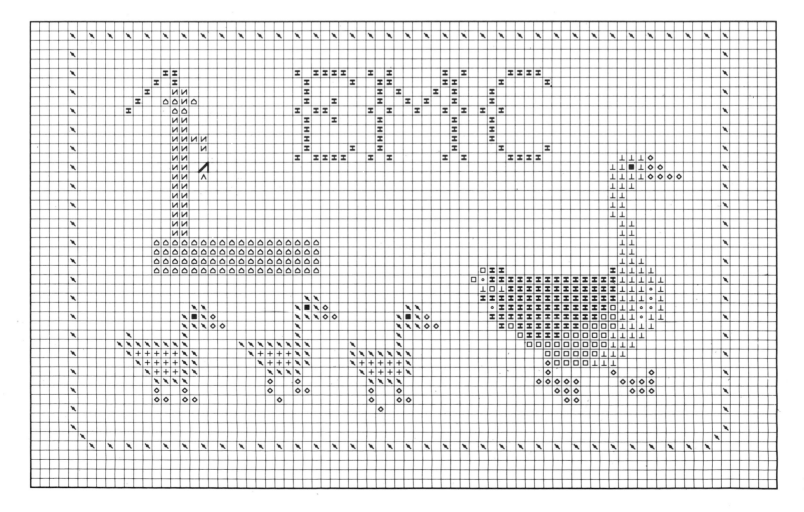

Photograph Frames

These delightful photograph frames will make an attractive addition to your home, whether displayed singly or together. Either of the two designs would make a lovely gift.

PHOTOGRAPH FRAMES

YOU WILL NEED

For the *Butterfly Watcher* frame, measuring
18cm (7in) approximately:

*22.5cm (9in) square of white, 14-count Aida fabric
18cm (7in) square piece of mounting board*

For the *Cat and Mouse* frame, measuring
24.5cm × 22.5cm (9¾in × 9in) approximately:

*28cm × 25.5cm (11in × 10in) of white,
14-count Aida fabric
24.5cm × 22.5cm (9¾in × 9in) of
mounting board*

For each frame you will also need:

*Stranded embroidery cotton in the colours given in
the appropriate panel
No24 tapestry needle
9cm (3½in) of white ribbon, 6mm (¼in) wide,
for a hanging loop
Thin white card to back the frame
Masking tape
Craft adhesive
Scalpel or craft knife*

●

THE EMBROIDERY

For each frame, prepare the fabric and stretch it in
a hoop or frame (see pages 6-7). Embroider the
border lines first, and then the rest of the design,
using two strands of thread in the needle for cross
stitching and one for the backstitching.

Leaving the basting stitches in at this stage,
as guidelines, gently press the finished embroidery
on the wrong side, using a steam iron.

MAKING THE FRAME

Carefully cut out a central window from the mounting board: the windows of the frames shown here
measure 7cm × 6.5cm (2¾in × 2½in), but
finished embroideries can vary slightly in size, so
check your own inner frame measurement.

Place your embroidery face down on a firm, flat
surface and, using the basting stitches as a guide,
position the mounting board on top of it. Next, mark
the cut-out on the fabric with a soft pencil. Remove
the basting stitches and, using a sharp pair of

scissors, make a small nick in the centre of the
fabric, and cut diagonally from the centre up to
each marked corner. Place the mounting board
over the fabric again, and fold the triangles of fabric
to the back of the board, securing them with masking tape. Next, fold in the outer edges of fabric,
mitring the corners and securing them with tape
(see page 9).

Using tape or craft adhesive, secure your chosen
photograph in position. Form the ribbon into a
loop, and secure it to the back of the frame with
adhesive, then cut a piece of white card to neaten
the back of the frame and secure this also with
adhesive.

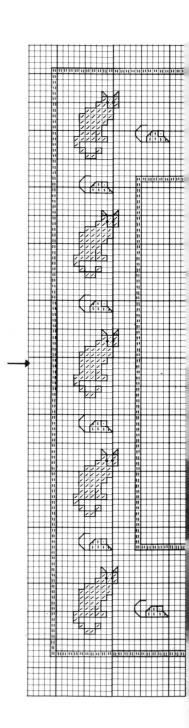

CAT AND MOUSE ▼	DMC	ANCHOR	MADEIRA
Black*	310	403	Black
⊞ Dark delft blue	798	146	0911
⦿ Peach	351	10	0214
⦾ White	White	2	White
⧄ Medium old gold	729	890	2210
⊡ Pale grey	415	398	1803

Note: backstitch outlines in grey and make eyes with french knots in black* (used for this only).

BUTTERFLY WATCHER ▼	DMC	ANCHOR	MADEIRA
Black*	310	403	Black
⊞ Very light carnation red	894	26	0413
⦿ Peach	353	9	0304
⦾ White	White	2	White
⧄ Medium old gold	729	890	2210
Steel grey*	414	400	1801

Note: backstitch outlines in steel grey* (used for bks only) and make eyes with french knots in black* (used for this only).

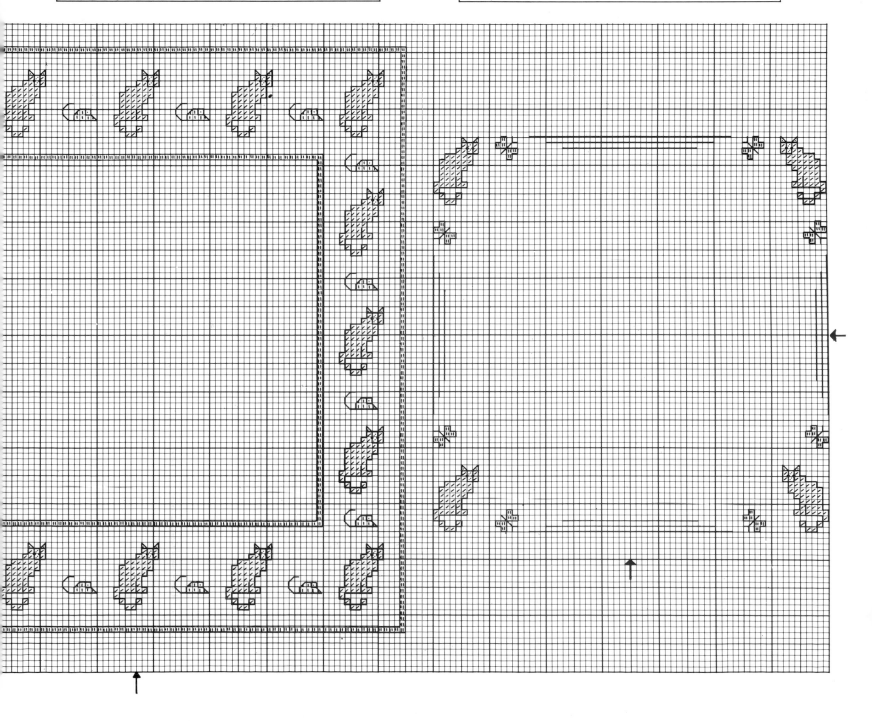

Seasonal Cushions

These beautiful lace-edged cushions, with their amusing cartoon-style cats, are simple to make and will brighten up any child's room, either scattered on the bed, or on a favourite chair.

SEASONAL CUSHIONS

YOU WILL NEED

For each cushion, measuring 20cm (8in) square,
excluding the lace edging:

30cm (12in) square of white,
18-count Aida fabric
22.5cm (9in) of contrasting fabric to back
your cushion
2m (2¼yds) of white lace, 2.5cm (1in) deep
Stranded embroidery cotton in the colours given in
the panels
No26 tapestry needle
Sewing thread to match the fabric
A cushion pad, 21.5cm (8½in) square

•

THE EMBROIDERY

Prepare the fabric, marking the centre lines of the
design with basting stitches, and mount it in a hoop
or frame, following the instructions on page 7.
Referring to the appropriate chart, complete the
cross stitching, starting at the centre and using two
strands in the needle throughout. Embroider the
main areas first, and then finish with the backstitching, this time using a single strand in the
needle. Steam press on the wrong side.

MAKING UP THE COVER

Trim the embroidery to measure 22.5cm (9in)
square. Using a tiny french seam, join the short
edges of the lace together. Run a gathering thread
close to the straight edge; pull up the gathers to fit
and, with the right side of the embroidery facing
and the lace lying on the fabric, baste the edging
to the outer edge, placing it just inside the 12mm
(½in) seam allowance. Adjust the gathers evenly,
allowing a little extra fullness at the corners.
Machine stitch the frill in place.

With right sides together, place the backing
fabric on top; baste and machine stitch around,
leaving a 15cm (6in) opening in the middle of one
side. Remove basting stitches; trim across the
corners, and turn the cover through. Insert the
cushion pad and slipstitch the opening to secure it.

SUMMER ▲		DMC	ANCHOR	MADEIRA
☐	Bright canary yellow	973	290	0105
●	Dark royal blue	796	134	0914
Ⅱ	Red	666	46	0210
■	Dark golden brown	975	310	2303
Ⅰ	Light topaz yellow	726	295	0109
•	White	White	2	White
C	Pale grey	415	398	1803
O	Very light peach	948	778	0306
=	Light pumpkin orange	970	316	0204
X	Medium lavender	210	109	0803
◢	Black	310	403	Black
V	Medium peach	352	9	0303
	Peach*	353	8	0304
∧	Light yellowy green	3348	264	1409

Note: outline eyes in black and nose and mouth in peach (used*
for backstitching only).

WINTER ▼		DMC	ANCHOR	MADEIRA
☐	Dark grey	413	401	1713
⦿	Light grey	318	399	1802
Ⅲ	Black	310	403	Black
⊟	Very light avocado			
	green	472	264	1414
◸	Dark forest green	986	245	1406
⦁	White	White	2	White
C	Pale grey	415	398	1803
◺	Very light peach	948	778	0306
	Peach*	353	9	0304
⊠	Medium peach	352	9	0303
⊙	Medium steel grey	317	400	1714
■	Very dark navy blue	939	152	1008
◪	Light yellowy green	3348	264	1409

Note: outline eyes in black and nose and mouth in peach* (used for backstitching only).

Spring Creatures

These delightful designs feature a goose and lamb, both surrounded by spring flowers; they have been made up as gift items in small porcelain and glass boxes, but would also make wonderful Easter cards or small pictures for childrens' rooms.

SPRING CREATURES

YOU WILL NEED

For the *Goose with violets*, set in a frosted glass bowl, 7.5cm (3in) in diameter:

15cm (6in) square of white, 18-count Aida fabric
Stranded embroidery cotton in the colours given
in the panel
No26 tapestry needle
Frosted glass bowl (for suppliers, see page 144)

For the *Lamb with blossoms*, set in an oval porcelain box, 8cm (3¼in) long:

15cm (6in) square of pale pink, 18-count Aida fabric
Stranded embroidery cotton in the colours given
in the panel
No26 tapestry needle
Pale pink oval porcelain box
(for suppliers, see page 144)

NOTE: If you are stitching both designs, you will only require one skein of each of the colours listed.

•

THE EMBROIDERY

For each design, prepare the fabric, marking the centre of the design with horizontal and vertical lines of basting stitches in a light-coloured thread. You can either set the fabric in a hoop or, for these small-scale designs, hold the work in the hand as you embroider. Start the embroidery from the centre and work outwards, working the cross stitches first and then finishing with the backstitching. Use one strand of embroidery cotton in the needle for both cross stitches and backstitching.

Wash the finished embroidery, if necessary, and lightly press with a steam iron. It is a good idea to leave the basting stitches in at this stage, as they will prove useful in helping you to centre your design in the lid.

ASSEMBLING THE LID

Place the finished embroidery face up on a firm, flat surface. Gently remove all parts from the lid of the trinket box. Use the rim of the lid and the basting stitches to centre the design. Using a hard pencil, draw a line on the fabric, around the outer edge of the lid, then cut along the drawn line, trimming the fabric to shape. Remove the basting stitches.

To assemble the lid, replace the clear acetate and place your design in the lid, with the right side to the acetate. Place the sponge behind your design. Push the metal locking disc very firmly into place, using thumb pressure, with the raised side of the disc facing the sponge. When the locking disc is tightly in position, use a little glue to secure the flock lining card to it.

GOOSE WITH VIOLETS ▶			DMC	ANCHOR	MADEIRA
Cross	Half Cross				
M		Mauve	554	96	0711
•		White	White	2	White
/		Very light grey	762	397	1804
X	\	Very light grey green	524	858	1511
P		Medium salmon pink	761	8	0404
O		Light pink	3713	48	0502
L		Light orange	402	1047	2307
Y		Light yellow	745	300	0111
		Medium grey green*	522	860	1513
		Medium orange*	722	323	0307
		Dark grey*	414	235	1801

Note: backstitch the stems on the wreath in medium grey green, the feet of the goose in medium orange* and the goose outline in dark grey* (starred colours are used for backstitch only).*

LAMB WITH BLOSSOMS ▶			DMC	ANCHOR	MADEIRA
Cross	Half Cross				
•		White	White	2	White
/		Very light grey	762	397	1804
X		Medium grey	318	399	1802
	I	Medium grey green	522	860	1513
P		Medium salmon pink	761	8	0404
Y		Light yellow	745	300	0111
S		Very light grey green	524	858	1511
		Dark grey*	414	235	1801

Note: backstitch the lamb outline in dark grey (used for backstitch only), and the flower stems in medium grey green.*

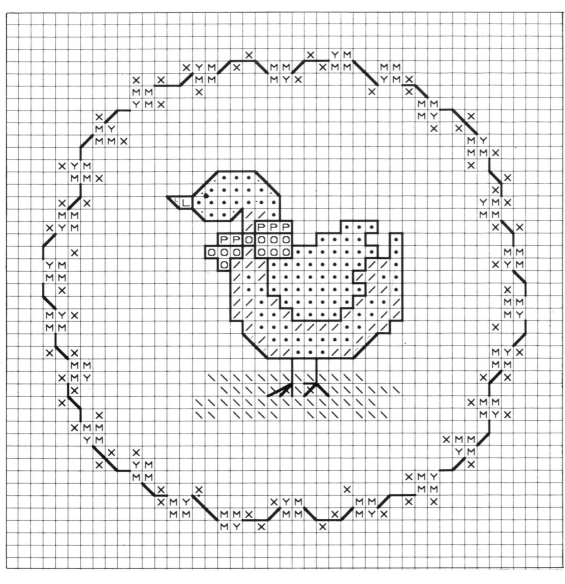

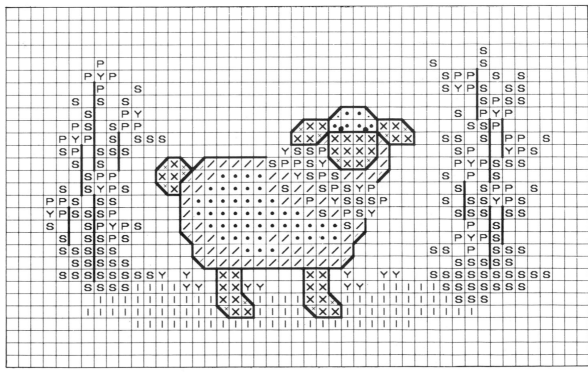

Serving Tray

When guests call in for morning coffee or afternoon tea, enchant them with this delightful tray – beautifully embroidered and mounted under glass. Alternatively, the design could be used for a small picture or a scatter cushion.

SERVING TRAY

YOU WILL NEED

For the tray, measuring 30.5cm × 40.5cm
(12in × 16in) with a 23cm × 30.5cm
(9in × 12in) oval cut-out:

*38cm × 48cm (15in × 19in) of pink, 14-count
Aida fabric
Stranded embroidery cotton in the colours given in
the panel
No 24 tapestry needle
Serving tray (for suppliers, see page 144)*

•

THE EMBROIDERY

Prepare the fabric and set it in a hoop or frame (see pages 6-7). Complete the cross stitch embroidery, using two strands of thread in the needle throughout. Finish by backstitching around the eyes, using one strand of black in the needle.

Gently steam press the finished embroidery on the wrong side.

ASSEMBLING THE TRAY

Gently remove all parts from the tray, following the manufacturer's instructions. Using a soft pencil, mark the supplied mounting board both ways along the centre to help you to position the board exactly in the middle of your embroidery. Place the embroidery face down on a firm, flat surface, and place the mounting board centrally on top. Fold the edges of the fabric over the board on all four sides, working first on one side and then the opposite side. Secure with one piece of masking tape on each side. When you are sure that the design is centred, turn in each corner to form a mitre, and secure firmly with masking tape. Next, finish securing the sides in the same way, ensuring that the fabric is stretched evenly. Insert the mounted embroidery into the tray, following the manufacturer's instructions.

TRAY ▶		DMC	ANCHOR	MADEIRA
⊙	Black	310	403	Black
∕	White	White	2	White
⦙	Pale grey	415	398	1803
C	Light steel grey	318	399	1802
‖	Steel grey	414	400	1801
V	Light antique pink	950	376	2309
✕	Pale brick red	758	868	0403
L	Light yellowy green	3348	264	1409

Note: use black to outline eyes.

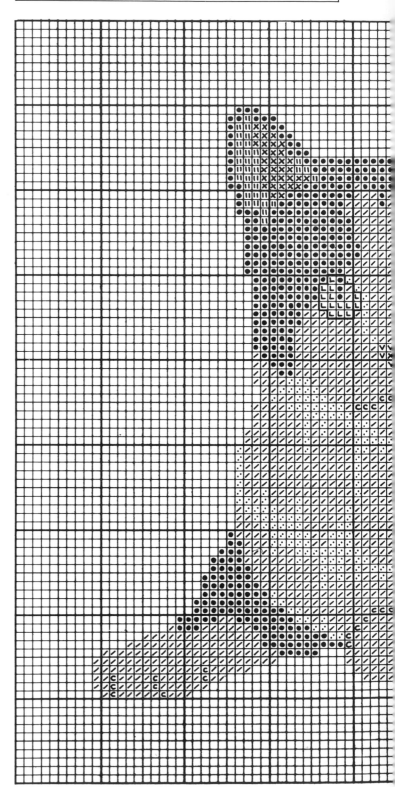

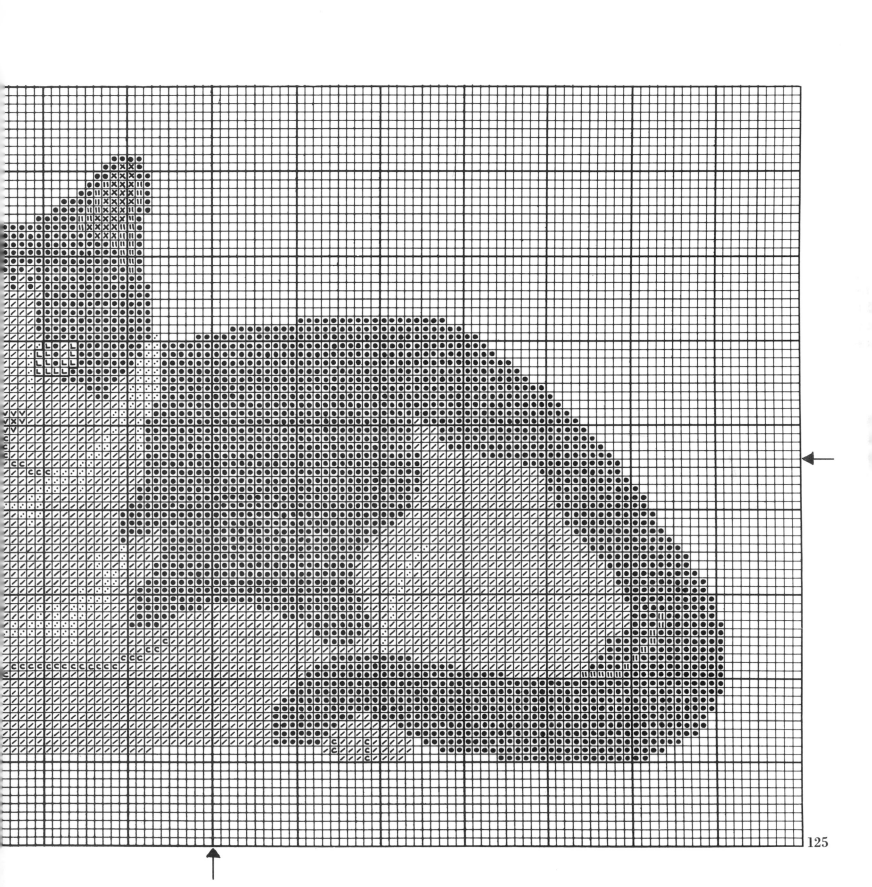

Tea Towels

The fabric used for these delightful tea towels has a reversible design and evenweave strips, intended for cross stitching, at both ends.
It is the width of two tea towels.

TEA TOWELS

For a pair of tea towels, each measuring
77.5cm × 45cm (30in × 18in):

50cm (19⅝in) of Zweigart 'Cats' fabric
Stranded embroidery cotton in the colours given in
the panel
No 24 tapestry needle
Sewing thread to match the fabric

•

THE EMBROIDERY

Fold and press the fabric to mark the dividing line
between the two tea towels, and cut along the foldline. Prepare the fabric (see page 6), marking the
centre point with a line of basting stitches across the
cross stitch band.

For each towel, set the fabric in a hoop or frame
(see pages 6-7). Complete the cross stitch embroidery, using three strands of embroidery cotton in the
needle throughout, and taking each stitch over one
fabric intersection. Finish with the backstitching,
this time using two strands of thread in the needle.
The repeats should stop 12mm (½in) short of the
raw edge at each side, to allow for the hem.

Gently press the finished embroidery on the
wrong side.

FINISHING THE TEA TOWELS

Pin and tack a 7mm (¼in) double hem on all four
sides. Machine stitch all around for a secure finish.

The border patterns have been designed with
mix-and-match in mind, so experiment with vari-
ations, interspersing the CATS lettering with paws,
for example, to make as many tea towels as you
wish.

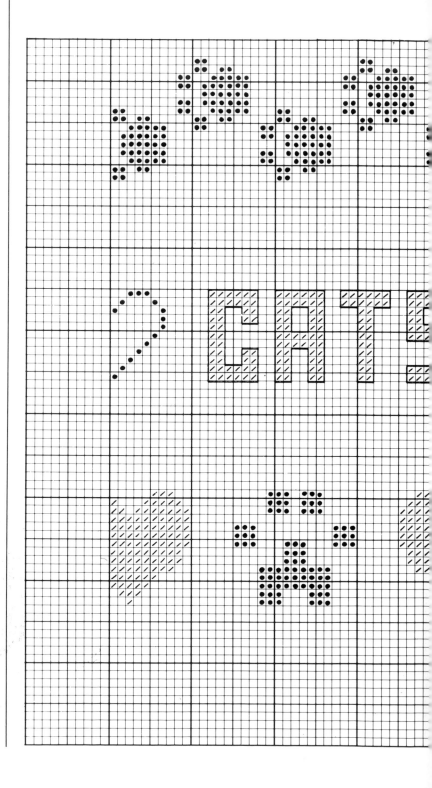

CATS ▲	DMC	ANCHOR	MADEIRA
● Black	310	403	Black
⁄ Red	666	46	0210

Note: backstitched outline in black.

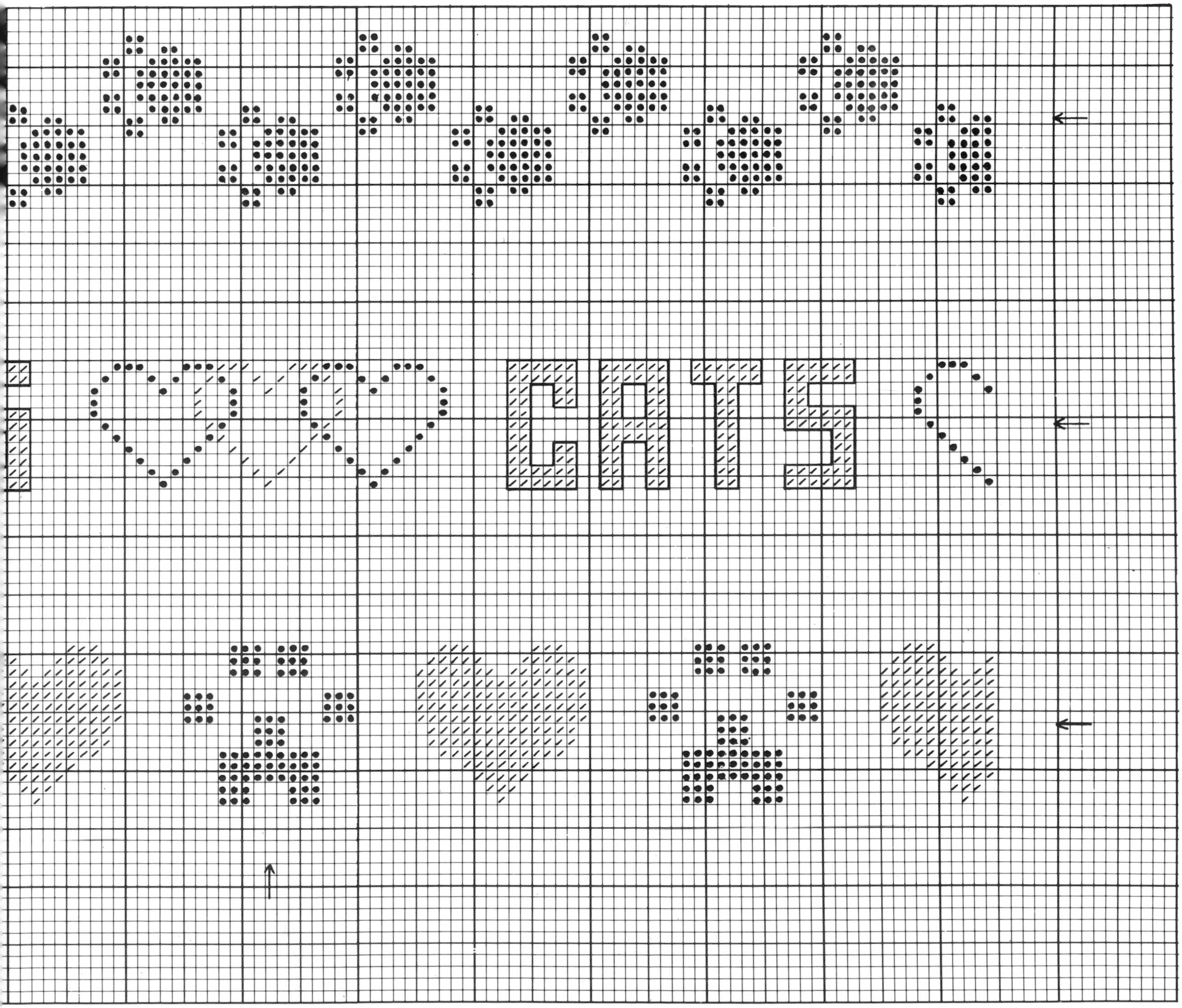

Porcelain Trinket Boxes

These beautiful porcelain trinket boxes make gifts which are both useful and decorative. They can adorn a dressing table, an occasional table, or even a mantelpiece.

PORCELAIN TRINKET BOXES

YOU WILL NEED

For each box:

15cm (6in) square of white, 22-count
Hardanger fabric
Stranded embroidery cotton in the colours given in
the appropriate panel
No26 tapestry needle
Trinket box (for suppliers, see page 144):
for Standing Bear, an oval box, measuring
8.5cm x 6cm (3¼in × 2¼in); for Heart Bear,
a heart-shaped box, measuring 7cm × 8cm
(2¾in × 3in); for Marching Bear, a circular box,
measuring 8cm (3in) in diameter

•

THE EMBROIDERY

All three designs are stitched in the same way and on the same type of fabric. If you wish to embroider all of the designs, you may be able to economize on fabric by using one large piece, remembering to allow sufficient space between each picture.

Prepare the fabric, marking the centre lines of the design with basting stitches, and mount it in a small hoop, following the instructions on page 6. Referring to the appropriate chart, and starting at the centre, complete the cross stitching, using a single strand in the needle throughout. Embroider the main areas first, and then finish with the back-stitching. If necessary, steam press on the wrong side.

It is a good idea to leave the basting stitches in at this stage, as they will prove useful in helping to centre your design in the lid.

ASSEMBLING THE LID

Place the finished embroidery face up on a firm, flat surface. Gently remove all parts from the lid of the trinket box. Use the rim of the lid and the basting stitches to centre the design. Using a hard pencil, draw a line on the fabric, around the outer edge of the lid, then cut along the drawn line. Remove basting stitches.

To assemble the lid, replace the clear acetate and place your design in the lid, with the right side to the

acetate. Place the sponge behind your design. Push the metal locking disc very firmly into place using thumb pressure, with the raised side of the disc facing the sponge. When the locking disc is tightly in position, use a little glue to secure the flock lining card to it.

STANDING BEAR ▼		DMC	ANCHOR	MADEIRA
I	Medium delft blue	799	140	0910
•	Christmas gold	783	307	2211
x	Dark topaz	781	308	2213
o	Dark mahogany	400	351	2305
	Dark beaver grey*	844	401	1810
■	Black	310	403	Black

Note: black used for backstitched mouth, dark beaver grey* for outlines.

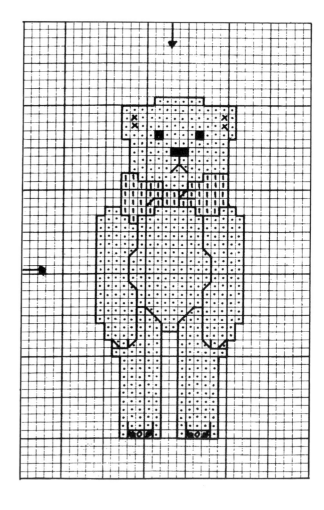

ALTERNATIVE USES

These designs are very simple and easy to stitch, and would make ideal first projects for a child who is interested in embroidery.

Rather than working on the rather fine fabric specified for the trinket boxes, however, it might be preferable to start on a fabric with a larger weave, say with 14 threads per 2.5cm (1in). In this case, the finished designs would, of course, be considerably larger and could not be used for the trinket box lids. Instead, the designs could perhaps be used for greetings cards (see page 46), or set in picture frames (see page 22).

Another way of using these designs would be to embroider them on preserve pot covers (ready made covers, trimmed with lace, can be purchased from specialist suppliers, see page 144).

To work out how much fabric you will need if you are changing the scale, count the number of stitches of your chosen design each way. Divide these numbers by the number of threads or blocks per 2.5cm (1in) of your fabric, then add an appropriate margin around the basic design size.

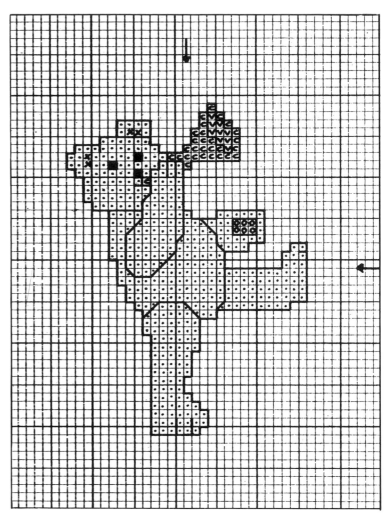

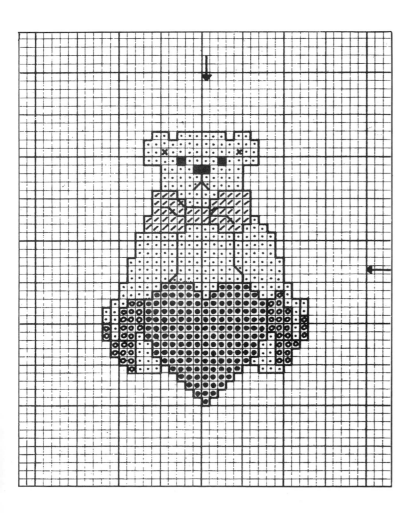

MARCHING BEAR ▲	DMC	ANCHOR	MADEIRA
• Christmas gold	783	307	2211
v Deep canary	972	303	0107
c Dark yellow	743	297	0113
x Dark topaz	781	308	2213
o Dark mahogany	400	351	2305
Dark beaver grey*	844	401	1810
■ Black	310	403	Black

Note: black used for backstitched mouth, dark beaver grey* for outlines.

HEART BEAR ◄	DMC	ANCHOR	MADEIRA
• Bright red	666	46	0210
• Christmas gold	783	307	2211
╱ Dark green	701	227	1305
x Dark topaz	781	308	2213
o Dark mahogany	400	351	2305
Dark beaver grey*	844	401	1810
■ Black	310	403	Black

Note: black used for backstitched mouth, dark beaver grey* for outlines.

Nightdress Case

Make this luxurious case to tuck away your nightie or pyjamas during the day. Lightly padded, trimmed with ribbon bows, and featuring a sleeping cat, it will look beautiful sitting on top of any bed.

NIGHTDRESS CASE

YOU WILL NEED

For a nightdress case, measuring 45cm × 33cm
(17¾in × 13in):

*94cm × 46.5cm (37in × 18½in) of pink,
14-count Aida fabric*
*94cm × 46.5cm (37in × 18½in) of lightweight
polyester batting*
*94cm × 46.5cm (37in × 18½in) of lightweight
cotton fabric for the lining*
*1.12m (44in) of ribbon, 2.5cm (1in) wide, in a
contrast colour*
*Stranded embroidery cotton in the colours given in
the panel*
No 24 tapestry needle
Sewing thread to match the fabric

●

THE EMBROIDERY

Prepare the edges of the fabric (see page 6); baste
a line across the width, 7.5cm (3in) up from the
bottom edge, to mark the baseline of the embroidery, and another 28.5cm (11½in) up from the
bottom edge (this marks off the area for the front
flap), then baste horizontal and vertical lines across
the embroidery area in the usual way.

Complete the cross stitching, working from the
centre and using two strands of embroidery thread
in the needle. Finish with the backstitching, made
with one thread in the needle. Gently steam press
the embroidery from the wrong side.

MAKING THE NIGHTDRESS CASE

Place the embroidered fabric face down on a flat
surface; carefully smooth the batting on top; pin
and baste the two together (12mm/½in seam
allowance); trim the batting back almost to the
basting line, and catch-stitch around the edge.

Make a single 12mm (½in) turning across the
width (not flap edge) of the fabric and baste. With
right sides facing, fold the pocket front section over
for 32cm (12½in); baste, and machine stitch to
form the pocket. Trim the corners and turn right
side out.

Make a single turning on the short edge of the
lining fabric and repeat as for the top fabric, but
do not turn the pocket to the right side.

With right sides of the top fabric and lining
together, baste and stitch around the flap, finishing

just above the side seams. Trim the corners and
turn the flap through to the right side. Slip the
lining into the pocket and slipstitch the top edges
together, easing the turning so that the stitching is
on the inside. Remove the basting stitches.

Cut the ribbon into two equal lengths; make two
bows and catch-stitch them to the flap of the nightdress case diagonally across the corners, as shown
in the photograph.

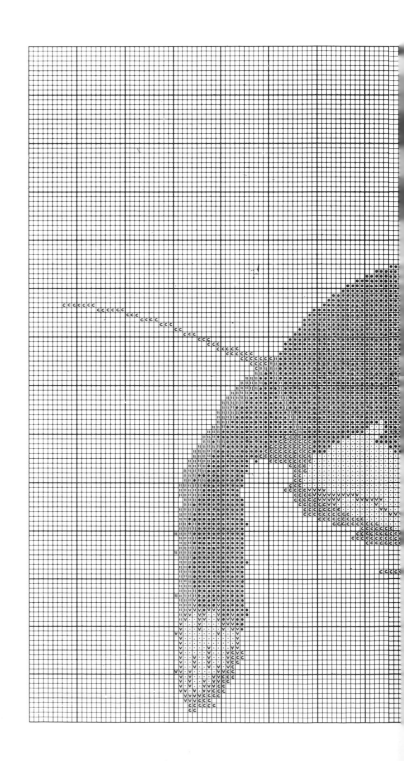

NIGHTDRESS CASE ▼		DMC	ANCHOR	MADEIRA
◢	Medium brick red	356	329	0402
◉	Black	310	403	Black
Ⅲ	Medium steel grey	317	400	1714
V	Pale grey	415	398	1803
•	White	White	2	White
C	Brown	3064	379	2310
X	Light steel grey	318	399	1802
◺	Steel grey	414	400	1801
P	Peach	353	9	0304
⊟	Pale brick red	758	868	0403

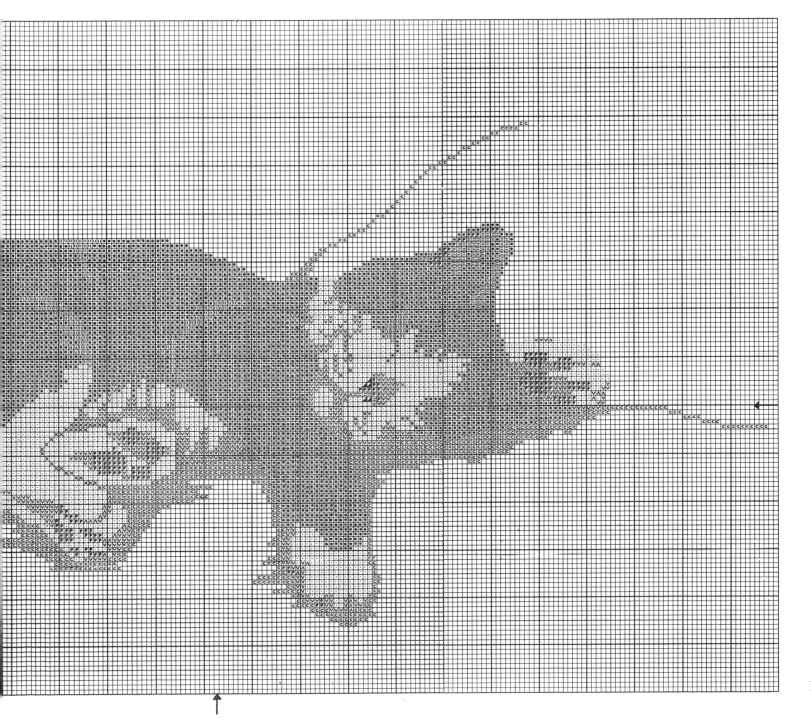

Kitten Paperweights

These beautiful paperweights make gifts which are both useful and decorative. They can be used to adorn a desk, a small table or even a mantelpiece.

KITTEN PAPERWEIGHTS

YOU WILL NEED

For each paperweight, *Sleepy Kitten,* an oval measuring 9.5cm × 6cm (3⅝in × 2⅜in); *Puss in Boot,* measuring 6.7cm (2⅝in) in diameter, and *Hat Cat,* a heart-shape measuring 6.5cm × 6cm (2½ × 2¼in):

*15cm (6in) square of white, 25-count Lugana fabric
Stranded embroidery cotton in the colours given in the appropriate panel
No26 tapestry needle
Paperweight (for suppliers, see page 144)*

•

THE EMBROIDERY

Each of these designs is stitched in the same way and on the same type of fabric. If you wish to embroider all three, you may be able to economize on fabric by using one large piece, remembering to allow sufficient space between each design.

Prepare the fabric and set it in a hoop (see pages 6-7). Complete the cross stitch embroidery, using one strand of thread in the needle throughout, and taking each stitch over one fabric intersection.

Gently press the finished embroidery on the wrong side.

ASSEMBLING THE PAPERWEIGHT

Place the embroidery face up on a firm, flat surface and use the paper template (provided with the paperweight) to draw around your design, ensuring that it is central. Cut the fabric to size and place right side down into the recess on the base of the paperweight. Place the paper template on to the reverse side of your embroidery. Next, peel the backing off the protective base and very carefully stick it to the base of the paperweight, ensuring that the embroidery and template do not move out of place.

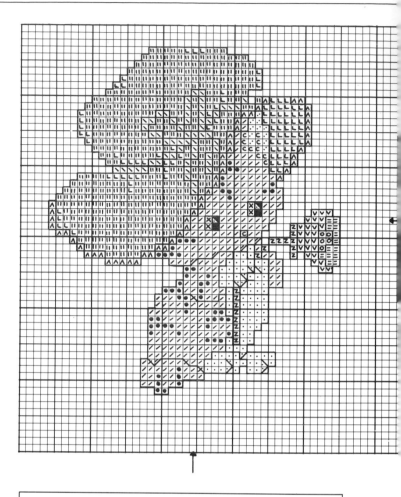

HAT CAT ▲		DMC	ANCHOR	MADEIRA
∧	Very dark cranberry	600	65	0704
L	Medium cranberry	602	62	0702
II	Light cranberry	604	60	0614
\	Dark delft blue	798	131	0911
O	Yellow	727	293	0110
=	Very light dusky rose	963	73	0502
V	Rose pink	962	52	0609
Z	Medium avocado green	3347	267	1408
C	Medium peach	352	9	0303
⦁	Light peach	754	6	0305
/	Very light beaver grey	3072	847	1805
●	Medium grey	414	400	1801
	Dark grey*	413	401	1713
⊠	Light yellowy green	3348	264	1409
•	White	White	2	White
■	Black	310	403	Black

Note: backstitch outline in dark grey* (used for outlines only).

SLEEPY KITTEN ▶	DMC	ANCHOR	MADEIRA
■ Black	310	403	Black
☒ Light yellowy green	3348	264	1409
• White	White	2	White
◉ Medium grey	414	400	1801
⬧ Very light beaver grey	3072	847	1805
⦁ Light peach	754	6	0305
C Medium peach	352	9	0303
⬓ Very light pearl grey	762	397	1804
Ⅱ Red	666	46	0210
Dark grey*	413	401	1713

Note: backstitch outlines in dark grey* (used for outlines only).

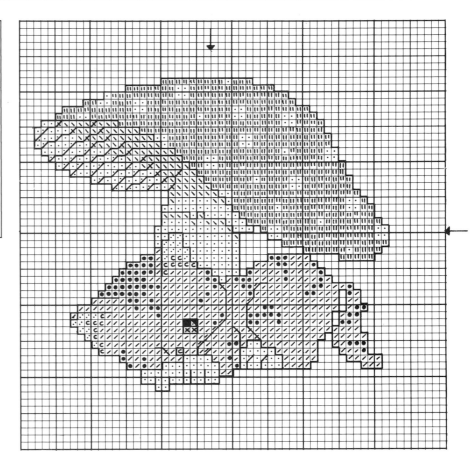

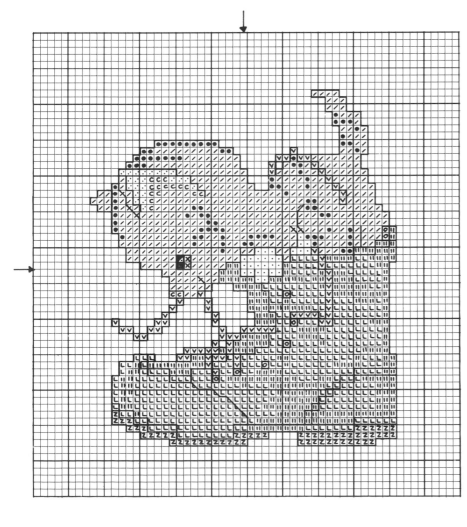

PUSS IN BOOT ◀	DMC	ANCHOR	MADEIRA
☒ Light yellowy green	3348	264	1409
■ Black	310	403	Black
• White	White	2	White
⦁ Light peach	754	6	0305
C Medium peach	352	9	0303
◉ Medium grey	415	398	1803
Very dark grey*	413	401	1713
⧄ Very light beaver grey	3072	847	1805
⋁ Golden wheat	3046	887	2102
Z Brown grey	3022	392	1903
L Very light tan	738	942	2013
Ⅱ Medium brown	433	371	2008
O Very dark coffee brown	898	380	2007

Note: backstitch in very dark grey* (used for bks only).

ꞮNDEX

∎

ACKNOWLEDGEMENTS

Thanks are due to the following suppliers, all of whom request that a stamped addressed envelope be enclosed with any enquiries.

The fabrics and threads were supplied by DMC, with the exception of the Wildlife Studies on pages 34-7, for which Coats Patons Crafts supplied fabric and threads; many of the items, including picture frames, the dressing table set, serving tray and trinket boxes, were supplied by Framecraft Miniatures Ltd, and the bib on pages 86-7 was supplied by Crafty Ideas, 'The Willows', Cassington Road, Eynsham, Witney, Oxon OX8 1LF.

SUPPLIERS

The following mail order company has supplied some of the basic items needed for making up the projects in this book:

Framecraft Miniatures Limited
372-376 Summer Lane
Hockley
Birmingham B19 3QA
England
Telephone 0121 359 4442

Addresses for Framecraft stockists worldwide
Ireland Needlecraft Pty Ltd
2-4 Keppel Drive
Hallam, Victoria 3803
Australia

Danish Art Needlework
PO Box 442, Lethbridge
Alberta T1J 3Z1
Canada

Sanyei Imports
PO Box 5, Hashima Shi
Gifu 501-62
Japan

The Embroidery Shop
286 Queen Street
Masterton
New Zealand

Anne Brinkley Designs Inc.
246 Walnut Street
Newton
Mass. 02160
USA

S A Threads and Cottons Ltd.
43 Somerset Road
Cape Town
South Africa

For information on your nearest stockist of embroidery cotton, contact the following:

DMC
(also distributors of Zweigart fabrics)

UK
DMC Creative World Limited
62 Pullman Road
Wigston, Leicester LE8 2DY
Telephone: 01162 811040

USA
The DMC Corporation
Port Kearney Bld.
10 South Kearney
NJ 07032-0650
Telephone: 201 589 0606

AUSTRALIA
DMC Needlecraft Pty
PO Box 317
Earlswood 2206
NSW 2204
Telephone: 02599 3088

COATS AND ANCHOR

UK
P.O. Box 22
McMullen Road
Darlington
Co. Durham, DL1 17Q
Telephone: 01325 365457

USA
Coats & Clark
PO Box 27067
Dept CO1
Greenville
SC 29616
Telephone: 803 234 0103

AUSTRALIA
Coats Patons Crafts
Thistle Street
Launceston
Tasmania 7250
Telephone: 00344 4222

MADEIRA

UK
Madeira Threads (UK) Limited
Thirsk Industrial Park
York Road, Thirsk
N. Yorkshire YO7 3BX
Telephone: 01845 524880

USA
Madeira Marketing Limited
600 East 9th Street
Michigan City
IN 46360
Telephone: 219 873 1000

AUSTRALIA
Penguin Threads Pty Limited
25-27 Izett Street
Prahran
Victoria 3181
Telephone: 03529 4400